Somme Story

Tyrone's Most Wanted Man: Andy Symington

Tony Ferguson

Third Edition

Published in 2025 by Misbourne Press

Copyright @Tony Ferguson

The author has asserted his moral right under the Copyright, Designs & Patents Act 1988
to be identified as the author of this work.

All rights reserved.

No part of this publication may be reproduced, copied, stored in a retrieval system or otherwise transmitted, in any form, or by any means without the prior written consent of the copyright holder, nor be otherwise circulated in any form of binding or cover other
than that in which it is published and without similar condition being imposed on the subsequent publisher.

ISBN: 978-1-918038-31-6

www.tonyfergusonauthor.com

An exhausted Royal Irish Fusilier coming from the Chemical Works at Roeux, 21st May 1917

Sketched by Sir William Orpen

The uniform worn by Private Andrew Symington 24168 1st Battalion Royal Irish Fusiliers

A story of two grandfathers and two grandsons. Three men spanning five generations

Cover Design by Annie King- Ferguson

Precis

Andy Symington volunteered to join the Royal Irish Fusiliers in 1916. Over the next seven years, he participated in the Battle of the Somme, the Irish War of Independence, and the Irish Civil War, a trilogy of military service experienced by fewer than sixty men, historians have estimated. His fighting career was a convulsion of contradictions: having been honourably discharged from the British army with a Silver War badge due to wounds and shellshock, he returned to Ireland and fought against the British (including the Black & Tans and Auxiliaries) for the nascent IRA, becoming the most wanted man in Tyrone in 1922; later in 1922, he switched sides again, became a lieutenant in the Free State army and fought against the IRA in the Civil War.

Meticulously researched, the book examines his life and times, casting light on some colourful characters like Geoffrey-Caiger Watson (an enigmatic RAF officer who survived a plane crash that killed his pilot on the penultimate day of the War); Woodbine Willie (a chaplain who crawled around No Man's land dispensing cigarettes and spiritual support to the wounded and dying); Tom Kettle, a gifted Irish academic and politician who not only lost his life but his place in history; and Mrs Mary Barbour who masterminded the Glasgow

Rent Strike from her scullery (forcing Lloyd George to introduce emergency legislation in her favour).

This book uncovers a previously suppressed story of mutiny and officer murder in the trenches and reveals how the press covered it up. It also exposes a cover up in the War Diaries, as Army High Command sought to distance itself from an ill-conceived attack which cost the lives of 385 men, many of them killed by their own side.

The work is in three volumes, collectively dedicated to the memory of Andy and focuses on the years 1916-23, the most remarkable years of this fighter's life. This first volume covers his time as a British soldier and examines the bloodiest battle in the Great War: the Somme. There is a strong human-interest undercurrent, from his early days in a family of ten in Fermanagh to the post war impact of alcoholism and shellshock (today known as Post Traumatic Stress Disorder, PTSD) on a tortured family life.

The second volume, when released, will examine Andy's role in the War of Independence against Britain. This period of his life was spent "on the run", harboured by close friends like the McLoughlins, and saw him become the most wanted man in Tyrone by the authorities. Volume three will cover his career as a Lieutenant in the Nationalist army during the darkest days of the Irish Civil War.

A century after the Somme, there emerged a divine twist when Andy's great grandson married the granddaughter of his second lieutenant and fellow trench warrior, a fact only uncovered during the research for this book. Ronan Ferguson and Stephanie Caiger-Watson owe their gift of life to the outrageous good fortune of Private Andy Symington and Second Lieutenant Geoffrey Caiger-Watson. It is miraculous to understand these two men fought together in the same dirty trench, in the same threadbare and beleaguered battalion…and both survived to create lineages that would converge in 2022.

I do not know the word for something bigger than a miracle. For now, I will call it a Findlay. Ronan and Stephanie's first born is simply that- a miracle of Life. His existence uniquely depended on the survival of both Andy and Geoffrey; two men that had the odds of reaching fatherhood very much stacked against them.

In commemorating my grandfather, I dedicate the endeavour to my grandson, Findlay Rafferty Ferguson.

Tony Ferguson
West Dene
June 8, 2022

Third edition May 2025

Dedication

To Findlay

March 7th, 2022

May he live a long and happy life

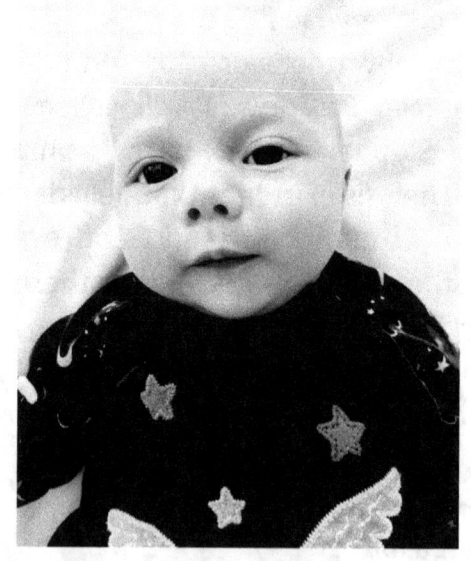

Contents

Precis

Dedication

Contents

1	INTRODUCTION	1
2	IT ALL STARTED IN TEMPO	27
3	THE SOMME	59
4	LIFE IN THE TRENCHES	77
5	LIONS LED BY ASSHOLES	100
6.	FIT FOR HEROES	117
7	THE MIRACLE OF LIFE	131
8.	MACROECONOMIC LEGACY	144
Dramatis Personnae		147
Acknowledgements		150
Epilogue (Neighbours)		151
Somme Story Reviews		169
Reviews by other Authors Photographs		172
Author		174
		179

1   INTRODUCTION

'Faugh-a-Ballaghs' was the soubriquet given to the Royal Irish Fusiliers back in the 19th century. Loosely translated from the Gaelic, it meant "Clear the way!" A bastardised version "Fuck a Bollocks" was more popular among the troops, intertwining as it did primitive Donegal Gaelic with English dialect. By the end of the war, the name "Faughs" (phonetically "Fawks") commanded the same respect as "the Die Hards", "the Black Watch" and "the Buffs." With many other regiments, they entered the grim brotherhood of battalions that had borne heavy losses.

On my first meeting with Jonathan Maguire, historian at the Regimental Museum in Armagh, he asked me if I knew which battalion my grandfather had served in. When I replied, "The First," he grimaced. "The unlucky one".

As the name "Faughs" implies, the rank & file of the regiment was largely recruited in Ireland, but English establishment dominated the command structure. The ranks of the First Battalion, Royal Irish Fusiliers expanded on 28th March 1916 with the enlistment of my grandfather, Private 24168: Andrew Symington. On that fresh Spring Day at the Mall in Armagh, he did not know the First Battalion was destined to suffer 83% casualties (killed or seriously wounded) with each recruit averaging three wounds. He had joined one of the most beleaguered units in the British army. When they tallied up the final score, the fourteen battalions of the Royal Irish Fusiliers would lose almost three thousand lives. Of those unfortunates, the First Battalion accounted for one thousand and fifty-eight.

On the other side of the ledger, Jonathan had calculated that any soldier from the First Battalion, who had spent a year in the trenches, would have killed at least fifty men. There is no doubt Andy Symington had blood on his hands.

I wrote the words above in June 2019 from a bedroom in Queen's College, Oxford. I had committed myself to a four-day lockdown in my son's old college to "kickstart" the book. A desperate attempt to draw inspiration from walls that incarcerated far more impressive intellects than mine, over many centuries. I promised my grandfather that one day, I would write a book about him. Over half a century later, it was time to settle the debt. The hour had struck.

I was carrying an obligation I did not know how to fulfil. My "writing" had been restricted to a sideline that occasionally supported my professional career, creating thought-pieces on technology in banking and insurance. I had never written a memoir, and in truth, I was ignorant about what constituted a "memoir." Queen's was an exercise in ordering my thoughts, identifying research that needed to be done, creating a structure and crucially, output. I wanted to leave with three thousand words. With that output, a title and structure, I felt I could say "I am writing a book" without feeling a complete fraud.

The epiphany struck on day three, in the dimming light of a long solstice evening. Thoughts were turning to a late dinner and decent claret, as I languidly thumbed the pages of the War Diary of the Faughs, the official chronicle of the First Battalion, Royal Irish Fusiliers. And there it was! In an appendix at the back. In the small print of a list of serving officers, it jumped out like a neon sign on Leicester Square.

"G Craiger- Watson". Second Lieutenant.

Oh my God!

Long hours spent on Ancestry.com had taught me not to assume. When you thought it must be the same person, the dispiriting coincidence would reveal itself. My daughter-in-law, Stephanie Caiger-Watson, had told me she thought her grandfather had fought in an Irish regiment in the First War. The name was slightly different (Caiger vs Craiger), which fostered doubt. I called my son, Ronan.

"Hey dad!" came his usual, jaunty greeting.

I was too excited to indulge in preliminaries. "Ro, Stephanie's grandfather, what was his Christian name?"

There was some muffled discourse as he consulted with his wife of one year.

"Jeffrey" was the reply.

"Is that Geoffrey with a G?" More muffled sounds at his end.

" Yes".

YES!! The jewelled keystone of the story had fallen into my trembling hands. Further due diligence would quickly confirm that "G Craiger-Watson" had won the Military Cross, as did Stephanie's grandfather. It was the same man. Geoffrey and my grandfather fought in the same "unlucky" battalion, roughly one thousand men in an army of some six million. It did not however prove that they had fought together, at the same time. Frustratingly, that took another two years to ascertain. The British Army Personnel Centre supports a Historical Disclosures Division which is based in Glasgow. As Geoffrey was an officer, quite detailed records of his army career and postings were maintained. In normal circumstances, my cheque for £30 would have released this treasure trove much earlier- unfortunately for me, Covid caused the facility to close and that, together with a backlog, led to the delay.

When the information arrived, it proved well worth the wait. Geoffrey's military career was laid bare, move by move, from joining the Sussex Yeomanry in 1914 up to, and including, his service in WW2 in Africa. One line recorded his transfer to the First Battalion of the Royal Irish Fusiliers on October 25th, 1916, before being invalided back to England on December 17th. He returned to the Faughs in February, before leaving to join the RAF in June 1918. In Chapter 7, "The Miracle of Life", we will examine Andy and Geoffrey's time spent together in trenches near Saillisel. Meanwhile, we return our attention to the Private from Tyrone.

A 24-year-old bachelor from a typical Catholic family of ten, Andy's act of volunteering was the first step in a military career contorted in contradiction. A military career that, in a congested seven years knew the horrors of the Somme; the depravity of the Black and Tan War and the despair of the Irish Civil War. His journey would personalise killing. He learned his trade at the Somme with a faceless enemy he did not know; onto the Tans and Auxiliaries, some of whom he knew but may not have liked and ending with people whom he knew and loved – his own republican kind. But they died just the same. He became hardened to killing and suffering. His emotional landscape bore the tortured memories of a Flanders field in February. A devastation in mud and rats, bloated bodies floating lifeless in putrid shellholes and the pervasive, asphyxiating stench of death and decay.

Why did a 24-year-old man sign up to go to war? There would have been no loyalty to King or Empire. Nor was it a fashionable thing to do in Ireland. Doctor Timothy Bowman identified that Irish recruitment to the army averaged a low two-per-one-thousand of eligible males, where the UK average per county stood at eight-per-thousand. I think partly the reason was that others in his family circle were doing so. Two brothers had already joined up. There was also the example set by his two brothers-in-law, Thomas and John McLoughlin. Andy was close to the McLoughlin family and would have looked up to them both. (As we shall cover in volume two, the McLoughlins sheltered Andy from the British in his days with the IRA).

Sergeant John McLoughlin was a career soldier who had already spent a decade in the army before he married Mary Symington in 1902. His service record included a shift for the Americans in their Spanish war. Andy would have seen his younger brother, Thomas McLoughlin, as even more of a role model. A talented footballer, Thomas had gone to Glasgow Celtic with Patrick McCaffrey for trials in 1901. A private in the Connaught Rangers in World War One, Thomas had a narrow escape at Messines where he had to be dug out of a trench after a German shell had hit it. Recounting the story when he came back to the Fivemiletown area on leave, in a sharp military uniform, he will doubtless have impressed Andy.

Like many young men before and since, he nurtured a desire for adventure, to escape the humdrum existence of working in a mill. Role models, peer pressure and thrill- seeking will have influenced his decision to take the King's shilling more so than the stable income on offer. In fact, he took a pay cut to quit the mill for the Western Front.

Having enlisted at the Royal Irish Fusiliers base in Armagh, Andy spent the war in the First Battalion until his honourable discharge in August 1917. As well as the Victory and British Empire medals, he was awarded the Silver War Badge, confirming his discharge because of wounds. A War Office certificate accompanied it. The latter document would start a lifelong prepossession with his "Correspondence." Life is a journey to insignificance. As we approach the exit, we invariably cling to a sense of value that is often misunderstood by the younger generations, but more often rendered worthless with the passage of time. And so Andy clung to his "correspondence" as a store of worth in his final years. He protected his correspondence in a small brown attaché case. Battered and decrepit with one of its two locks broken, this little case resided majestically on top of his wardrobe.

Once, to sate juvenile inquisitiveness in my grandfather's absence (almost certainly in the pub), my abiding memory was of the musty smell of decaying paper. Paper confined to a restricted space for many years. Yet these artefacts held such value for him. He alone knew the cost of that Silver War badge certificate, because he alone knew what he had given. Physically and emotionally. And pay for it he did with every shellshocked migraine and tormented memory over 50 years. The rest of his life, he slept with the light on in his bedroom. Darkness made him acutely aware of every sound. In the darkness, his mind would roll back to sentry duty in the trench. Every peculiarity of sound was processed in the heightened level of concentration and vigilance that comes when the stake is your life. Memories of war persisted to pluck the strings of a tortured mind. In daylight, he would at times sit with his hands joined. As he stared into mid space, he would revolve his thumbs like he was charging the battery of dim recollection. When he was in the house, I remember how he often took to tying a tight train of knots in an old bandage, which he would wind tightly around his head. It was if he were binding the very pieces of his head together, fearful that his own thoughts might escape into the room.

Discharged from the British Army in August 1917, Andy returned to County Tyrone to find things radically changed. The 1916 Easter Rising and the British military handling of its aftermath had galvanised the Irish republican aspiration. As if to stoke the flames, the British had created a new force- the hated Black and Tans, who entered the Irish arena in February 1920. There was a longstanding myth that the British had emptied their gaols to create the Black and Tans. While this is untrue, the uncomfortable reality is that a cadre of Black and Tans were released from secure mental institutions where they were being treated for various mental illnesses, a by-product of their time spent in the trenches. Paid ten shillings per day plus bonus and a pension, one can understand their enthusiasm to take employment where little was available in a stagnant British economy. Their task was to support the beleaguered Royal Irish Constabulary (RIC) but their mental state, experience, and lack of training made them wholly unsuitable for a policing role. Ill disciplined, they were involved in many barbaric outrages.

Of course, the enemy did not just include the Black and Tans. From October 1920, the British government had also created the B Specials, a quasi- military group of Protestant part-time volunteers. Well-armed and with the advantage of local knowledge of terrain and people, they struck fear in the Catholic communities in the secularly discriminated North of Ireland. Coalisland was one such area and Coalisland was where Andy's family lived and to where Andy returned. A third enemy force was the Auxiliaries. This was a unit recruited from former officers who had served in WW1. Andy had no advantage over these guys. Like him, they were experienced fighting men, battle hardened in the same theatres and quite ruthless. Although their tour in Ireland lasted less than one year, they were the most feared of all.

Having joined the nascent Irish Republican Army (IRA), Andy's military career was to move in a contradictory direction. Not just that having served the British he was now fighting against them; there was also the contradiction of the IRA accepting him into their ranks. This man had spilled his own blood in voluntary service of the King and had a legion of dead comrades pall bearing his mental baggage. He had been away from Coalisland for two years and that would have bred suspicion. His younger brother, George, another ex-soldier, also returned to the town. He had no IRA involvement. Usually, the IRA were highly suspicious of former servicemen whose attractiveness as experienced fighting men they would reject for fear that they were British agents.

"These boys you keep outside the tent" was the feeling of the IRA hierarchy.

Moreover, there was a natural jealousy in fitting them into the IRA command structure, as this meant displacing loyal but less experienced men. Historians like Con Mulhall estimated that only about sixty returning ex-servicemen were admitted into the IRA. Many of these became drill sergeants, allowed to teach the basic disciplines but precluded from active combat engagements. My grandfather's long-time neighbour, Joe Donaghy, was also one of the sixty. Sixty is a paltry number out of over 150,000 Irishmen who were war veterans. The remarkable thing with Andy was that not only was he admitted into the IRA, but during the War of Independence, he became the British Army's most wanted man in Tyrone. A metamorphosis from Honourable Discharge to Dishonourable Charge, but only if they could catch him!

Andy joined the Coalisland Battalion of the IRA in 1919, his inclusion facilitated by his pre-war friendship with the Brigadier, Bob Crawford. He was soon promoted to sergeant and put in charge of musketry, before joining a Flying Column in the Second Northern Division in late 1921. The War of Independence really intensified for the Northern Divisions after the Truce and reached its zenith after the signing of the Anglo-Irish Treaty. From

January to May 1922, Tyrone and Belfast were the two most rebellious hotspots in Ireland.

Outside Ulster, the relatively successful prosecution of the War of Independence ended with the truce in July 1921. A period of intense negotiation led by Lloyd George and Michael Collins respectively saw the signing of the Anglo-Irish Treaty, which effectively ended 120 years of direct British rule over twenty-six of Ireland's thirty-two counties. Thus, the creation of the Irish Free State with the consequent partitioning of six of the remaining counties in Ulster, a grouping which included the catholic majority counties of Fermanagh and Tyrone.

Notwithstanding that Andy was born in Fermanagh (Lisnaskea) and baptised and raised in the Tempo area, before the family featured in Tyrone (Shambles Lane, Dungannon) for the 1911 Census, his next move in his military career is a convulsion of contradictions. With republican Tyrone and Fermanagh feeling abandoned and sold short, why would Lieutenant Andrew Symington join Michael Collins Nationalist army and turn his guns on the IRA, his erstwhile comrades? A century later, one can only surmise at his reasons, based on the balance of probabilities. As an economist, I acknowledge the prevailing economic conditions of the time. As the armies demobilised after the war, there were over three million men released back into the labour market, in a period when the labour market was contracting in a stagnant economy. Wartime production demand had ceased and there was nothing to take up the slack. Thus, there was deflation and 1921 recorded the highest rate of unemployment ever seen in the UK at 23.4%.

In some ways, this was a move back into the mainstream as six hundred of the National Army's three thousand officers were ex-British servicemen from World War One. Indeed, so were half of the fifty-three thousand rank and file (as estimated in May 1923). Michael Collins' decision to double their pay as part of his recruitment drive was certainly successful, and I believe this was a factor in Andy's decision. However, it was not the only factor, nor was it the weightiest. As we shall examine in Book Two of the series, the Joint Northern Offensive of 1922 saw the command of the Second Northern Division taken over by men from Cork and Kerry. Although successful fighters, these leaders had little understanding of local conditions and lacked Andy's military experience. Anti-Treaty, they did not gain Andy's respect. Unlike Michael Collins, whom Andy had met a few times.

It was still the hardest decision Andy ever faced. To understand its enormity, one must appreciate that Fermanagh and Tyrone were at the heart of the dilemma in the Treaty negotiations. The British had wanted to create a new Northern state possessing economic and geographic viability (encompassing the lucrative linen industry), but could not find a boundary, which included Fermanagh and Tyrone as a Protestant majority. Those two counties simply flummoxed the British, eloquently summed up by Winston Churchill in February 1922:

"The complete map of Europe has changed...but as the deluge subsides and the waters fall short, we see the dreary steeples of Fermanagh and Tyrone emerging once again."

Churchill's words were in the context of four empires having collapsed because of the war, several countries being abolished, and new ones formed as boundaries were redrawn in the Allied carve up...yet Tyrone and Fermanagh remained defiant and unsolved.

From the Irish perspective, Collins and Griffiths knew that to abandon Fermanagh and Tyrone was disastrous for the Republican narrative. It would seismically split the IRA, notwithstanding the impossibility of a united Ireland. Northern Ireland was already created ahead of the treaty negotiations, albeit not defined geographically. The British offered a self-governing Free State as a Dominion within the British Commonwealth. It was the most heinous option, with de Valera sniping from the sidelines...

Forced into an impossible position by Lloyd George, Collins had the choice to accept the Treaty or enter a full-scale war with Britain within seventy-two hours. This was the demographic equivalent of Britain declaring war on Manchester. Knowing intimately the state of men, munitions, and military readiness (or lack of them), and aware that the British had three million battle-hardened troops seeking employment, Collins reluctantly accepted the Treaty. He was likely gambling he could sell it at home as a device to subsequently achieve the desired endgame. A steppingstone to an independent Irish Republic. This was a gamble as deadly as any Russian roulette. It was a gamble which Collins knew might cost him his life. As they put pen to paper, Lord Birkenhead expressed his concern that he was signing away his political career. Collins replied prophetically: "I am worried I am signing my death warrant".

They signed the Treaty on a wintry 6th of December 1921 in Heatherden Hall. Today, it is better known as Pinewood Studios. It is four miles from Gerrards Cross where I now continue my English exile. I remember having dinner at Lambeth Palace with John Prescott (former Labour Deputy Prime Minister under Tony Blair).

We were talking about the importance of humour in politics, and it cued me to recount a tale I had read on the treaty negotiations. Churchill was relaying in a drab monotone a list of incidents where IRA activity had breached the truce. Collins scribbled a note, which he passed across to Eamonn Duggan.

"Can we explain these?"

Duggan wrote a one-word answer: "No"

On reading the response, Collins slammed his fist down on the table and shouted:

"For God's sake, man, get to the point!"

The outburst was so unexpected that all delegates, including Churchill, broke into laughter. Deflection accomplished. John Prescott told me he had seen the actual note, as it had been retained in the government archive.

Collins' dramatic prophecy of his death all too soon became reality. Three of the Irishmen present that night were Michael Collins, Secretary of State for Finance, Arthur Griffiths, Secretary of State for Foreign Affairs and Erskine Childers, Delegation Secretary. Within eleven months, they were all dead.

The restricted extent of Irish independence, the oath of allegiance to the Crown and losing Fermanagh and Tyrone were three factors that condemned the Treaty. Ireland descended into the darkness of Civil War. With the benefit of historical detachment, I now realise the significant role played by De Valera in pushing Ireland into Civil War. While Collins was trying to sell the Treaty to his comrades as giving "the freedom to win freedom," De Valera was touring the country making emotional and incendiary speeches. He majored on the oath of allegiance to the Crown, dismissing it as something no Irishman had ever done in 700 years. His absence from the negotiations now looks like he was more concerned with "winning the peace" and discrediting Collins.

It is noteworthy how far opinion in Ireland had shifted in seven short, if tumultuous years since the outbreak of World War One. Before the declaration, the most popular politician in Ireland was unquestionably John Redmond. MP for Waterford City and Chairman of the Irish Parliamentary Party, he opened a bridge in Waterford in February 1913. To the sounding of foghorns, a gathering of over twenty-five thousand people greeted him. The 1912 Home Rule Bill had just passed its third reading in the House of Commons. The leading nationalist involved, his name synonymized Home Rule. They heaped accolades upon him. The United Irish League proclaimed its "unswerving loyalty to Redmond" and none other than the Waterford Pig Buyers Association announced it was "proud to be represented in the English Parliament by a man of such wonderful genius and tact".

The Government of Ireland Act was duly passed in 1914 but promptly suspended because of the war. Expecting a brief war before the Grail of Home Rule, Redmond called for Irishmen to support the British Empire by enlisting. He hoped mutual service in a common cause would heal divisions between unionist and nationalist. The vast majority of the paramilitary Irish Volunteer Force (which Redmond also led) followed his persuasion and joined the British army.

A small rump refused, and this reluctant cadre would provide the determination, planning and execution of the 1916 Easter Rising. The Law of Unintended Consequences would once again shake hands with a one dimensional British general. Maxwell's brutal handling of the aftermath drove Ireland into republicanism. The extent of the political earthquake appeared in December 1918 when the elections gave Sinn Fein a landslide while reducing Redmond's Irish Party to a meagre six seats. In the south of Ireland, the only seat held was Wexford, which also held his body, Redmond having died earlier that year. He chose to spend eternity in his hometown in preference to Glasnevin cemetery. The ensuing War of Independence would complete Ireland's quickfire transition from Home Rule aspirant to Free State.

Against this backdrop, Andy Symington, Fermanagh born and resident of Tyrone, rode his bicycle to Black Lion in Cavan and completed his attestation into the fledgling Irish Nationalist Army. It was the 16th of May 1922. Captain Symington had sided with the Free Staters. As a member of W Company, 18th Battalion, he marched into Custume Barracks in Athlone for the symbolic British withdrawal and handover to the Saorstat. His personal chamber of horrors was about to be extended...

My grandfather and I were close. We shared a bedroom for several years up to his death. I knew him as a quiet and intensely private man. He was a man often imprisoned in the solitary confinement of his thoughts. Thoughts based on experiences too horrific to understand, never mind gratuitously share with a juvenile grandson. Prone to fits of melancholy, he sometimes recounted the story of his lying wounded in No Man's Land among several colleagues as the overworked and under-fire stretcher bearers picked up an officer nearby. Amid the carnage, the officer croaked an order: "Pick up Symington- he's a good 'un". This act of benevolent discrimination saved my grandfather's life. But at the tortuous opportunity cost of his pals left to lie and die. He recalled the episode, not in gratitude, but in guilt. The guilt of the survivor was a burden he carried throughout his life. Given the epiphany at Queen's College in Oxford, an intriguing question now surfaces in the present day: who was that officer? Could it have been Second-Lieutenant Geoffrey Caiger-Watson MC? Could Geoffrey have saved Andy's life? In Chapter Seven, "The Miracle of Life", we answer that question.

Granda fostered our relationship with minor acts of kindness, mostly unconditional, sometimes in return for an errand. Ten Woodbine from the side door of Crilly's Bar in Brackaville being typical. The only reprimand I can remember receiving from him concerned my slowness in hanging up holy pictures. Particularly when compared to a full colour page of Jimmy Greaves, surgically extracted from my father's copy of Football Monthly in 1963. "You wouldn't hang up a picture of Our Lady as quick!" Such was his tolerance that Greavesie stared at us for a full season before being confined to the dustbin when I transferred my allegiance to Arsenal.

One of my earliest memories of him was when he used a scythe to cut the grass in the field adjoining our house. With a rhythmic swish, the grass fell like a line of soldiers under machine gun fire. Fond memories are always bathed in sunshine, and I can see him now, slowly but methodically, scything his way through the field on a balmy morning. The grass would be allowed to lie for a few days to dry, before being turned to allow the other side to be exposed to the sun. A couple of weeks later, the most exciting phase of the process when I would assist him in building the haystack! I would stand on top, trampling each forkful of hay that granda reached up, the excitement mounting the further I was elevated from the ground. Eventually, he would pass up a square sheet of tarpaulin, which I would use to cover the top. This would later have ropes fed through each corner and attached to house bricks to weigh down the stack and provide protection from the wind. It would then be time to get me back onto terra firma and granda would drive his fork into the side of the hay, so giving me a foothold and then use another to graduate my descent. Over sixty years later, the smell of dry hay and the sense of pride in what we had created are fresh in my memory.

One educational residue of trench life was a smattering of pidgin French, which he would occasionally flex when he knew I was studying French as an eleven-year-old at grammar school.

"Common tally vu?" would be rasped out as grandfather cemented his place with grandson in the multi-lingual, intellectual hierarchy of the family.

Granda had a military bearing with a ramrod straight back and sported a full head of grey hair right until his death in May 1970. He had clearly been a very handsome man. A legacy of army discipline, or maybe just his nature, but he was conceited about his appearance and always very well dressed. Others described him as "dapper" and indeed this trait carried through to all his children. His eldest son, the cravatted George Joe, perhaps stretched it to "flamboyant". His youngest son Patsy was the closest replica, with his well-polished shoes, neatly seamed trousers, and a keen eye for a tailored sports jacket. Even his middle son Aloysius, the roughest of the three diamonds, cut a well-tailored figure in later years. His daughters Emma and Madeleine inherited the gene and were two elegant, stylish women throughout their lives.

Returned to civilian life, Grandad took succour in alcohol, which sometimes involved him in deeds that damaged his self-respect. He regularly pawned his war medals in the compulsive pursuit of his next drink. A physical legacy of the trenches was the searing headaches he regularly suffered. His antidote was the futile yet comical action of knotting a handkerchief around his head, as previously noted. However, the bigger damage was internal. He had blood on his hands. Jonathan Maguire, the regimental historian based at the

Royal Irish Fusiliers Museum in Armagh, has calculated that every surviving infantry soldier would have killed an average of fifty enemy soldiers. Some killed many more. Andy Symington was a warrior condemned to live with what he had done and what he had experienced. What he had seen and survived.

Post-Traumatic Stress Disorder (PTSD) had not been baptized with a name, as doctors had not recognised it as a condition throughout my grandfather's life. But look back through the lens of modern medical science at the afflictions that befell trench warriors, and it becomes clear and obvious. Stories abound of soldiers who had bayoneted men in the face developing hysterical tics of their own facial muscles. Stomach cramps seized men who had knifed their foes in the midriff. Recurring nightmares of being unable to withdraw bayonets from the enemies' bodies persisted long after the killing. The nightmares might occur 'right in the middle of an ordinary conversation' when 'the face of a Boche that I have bayoneted, with its horrible gurgle and grimace, comes sharply into view', one infantryman explained. Charles Myers coined the term "Shellshock" in 1915 to define such intrusions of memory, as well as shivering, crying and intense anxiety.

The Western Front Association holds the World War One pension record cards that have survived. They actually singled out Andy Symington's record card as being highly unusual as it identified "shellshock" as a cause of discharge. See the Appendix.

Government figures subsequently revealed that around eighty thousand veterans were institutionalised with shellshock after the war. One of these was the renowned poet and composer, Ivor Gurney. Born in Gloucester, he had already published the anthology "Severn & Somme" before being gassed at Passchendaele in September 1917. He suffered a nervous breakdown and was discharged from the army in October 1918 with "deferred shellshock". He wrote over two thousand poems including a moving second anthology, "Wars Embers". His "Gloucestershire Rhapsody" is a beautiful piece of nostalgic music, which contrasts with the demons that he was fighting in his head. It was one fight he could not win and in 1922, he succumbed and was committed to the City of London Mental Hospital. He was never released and died in 1937.

Two hundred thousand Irishmen volunteered to fight in WW1. Thirty-five thousand were killed. Some six thousand Irish soldiers were declared insane- so much for reaching the sunny uplands of Peace. Probably the most famous shellshock victim was the poet Siegfried Sassoon. Described as "suicidally brave" and affectionately nicknamed "Mad Jack", he won the Military Cross, which he promptly threw in the Mersey in disgust! Thanks to the Great War, the word "shellshock" remains in the common vernacular but no longer exists in medicine. Today they call it PTSD. Andy Symington silently carried the cross of PTSD for over 50 years.

As for his alcoholism, I acknowledge the negative impact this sometimes had on domestic and family life. My childhood memories are peppered with fierce arguments, shouting, dark sulking moods, and a lack of tranquillity. I absolutely exonerate him. So many trench survivors sought respite in alcohol. In the prescient prose of the Iranian poet, Omar Khayyam:

"Ah, my Beloved, fill the cup that clears today of past regrets and future fears…"

The path from battle to bottle was very well trodden. Understandably.

In the darkest hours, there was also amusement. My grandmother, Lizzie (nee Forker), earned the description as "a woman who could have saved a bit of money". Her challenge was to keep it from the marauding fingers of her husband, particularly in the run up to Pension Day when funds were low, and thirsts were raging. Her stash had to be concealed. On one occasion, she buried the biscuit tin and pecuniary contents in the field. As an additional precaution, the chosen burial plot lay squarely in an area accessible to, and patrolled by, our tethered cow. My grandparents habitually kept one or two cattle in a byre behind the house. This cow did not like my grandfather and had previous convictions for assault, causing Andy to adopt a prudent policy of giving it as wide a berth as possible. Satisfied with the impregnability of her defensive strategy, my granny came out some time later on a routine patrol to inspect her handiwork. The sight of the severed tether brought shock, consternation, frustration, and dismay. The rope had been cut in an act of terrorism. Worse still, three mysterious disappearances- the cow, the contents of the biscuit tin and my granda!

Sadly, my granny took her revenge. She reached the end of her tether and buried my grandfather's war medals in an unmarked grave somewhere in the garden. Despite extensive excavation of the rhubarb patch, to this day they have never been found.

2   IT ALL STARTED IN TEMPO

Tempo is a hamlet in the east of Fermanagh close to the Tyrone border. Lying at the foot of Brougher Mountain (a 317-metre hill which to describe as a "mountain" is stretching it), Tempo enjoys a picturesque, rural setting. The eponymous river joins with the Colebrook before flowing into Upper Lough Erne just to the southeast of Enniskillen. The B80 Cullion Road, which also serves as the Main Street, bisects the settlement. Over the past 150 years, little has changed.

Two churches dominate the main street. Atop a hill at the southern end is the Church of Ireland, an imposing grey building. An impressive stairwell leads up from the street below. Two hundred yards further north on the same side of the road stands the Church of the Immaculate Conception, ministering to the needs of the Roman Catholic community. With scant respect for the labours of the genealogist, both churches contain a sizeable cadre of Symingtons. Illiteracy added bastardised variations. Simonton, Symonton, Syminton, Symengton, Siminton and Symmington, among others. The Plantation of Ulster introduced them as Scottish Presbyterians before a recalcitrant decided to "kick with the left foot". William Symington, my great-great-grandfather (commonly known as Willie), was born in 1831. I cannot confirm that he started the Catholic strand of Tempo Symingtons. I mention it because "William" was not a popular Christian name for Catholics. Another genealogist grumble was the custom of the parish priest to attempt Latinisation of the church records- thus my great-great-grandfather regularly appeared as "Giulelmi Simonton".

Between the churches across the road stands Campbells Bar, catering to more earthly requirements for over 200 years. It carries the reputation of the most haunted bar in Fermanagh. Ecumenical relations were not always harmonious, and the Freemans Journal of 19th Sept 1896 recorded the events of the "Tempo Riot". A drunken protestant mob, led by one John Symington, inflicted severe damage to twenty catholic houses in Tempo. Joseph Maguire led the drunken catholic mob in resistance. The drafting of nineteen policemen from Enniskillen and district eventually restored order. One way to "bring the house down" on August Fair night! With eight children under the age of fourteen, such sectarian toxicity will have been a factor in my great grandfather, Matthew Symington's decision to move to Tyrone. The primary driver will have been economic, however.

It was in the Catholic church in Tempo that Matthew Symington took the hand of Sarah Graham on the 26th of November 1881. Education bypassed the common man in Victorian Ireland, and both Matthew and Sarah were illiterate. The phonetic spelling of Simonton in the Parish Register was a strong clue. The 1911 Census brutally confirmed the fact. This was no disgrace, per se. Illiteracy was widespread. Ireland boasted the highest illiteracy rate in the UK at 13.2% of males, outstripping Scotland at 3.4% and England/Wales at 2.8%. Even 30 years later, the pressures of raising a family had kept literacy out of reach for Matthew and Sarah. Although my grandfather and his younger siblings could read and write, learning was confined to the school. Typical houses were single story, two rooms, and lit by the dim flickerings of pungent paraffin lamps. Heavily congested with large families, they were not conducive to encouraging homework, study, or any reverse transfer of literacy. In these cramped and cloistered conditions, Matthew and Sarah would raise a family of ten children between 1882 and 1899. The cast (in order of appearance): Thomas, Mary, Ellen, James, John, Matt, Andrew, Sarah Jane, George and Margaret.

As a 25-year-old shoemaker, Matthew Symington would have represented "a good catch" for Sarah. Particularly as Sarah was in the socially disadvantaged position of carrying another man's child, to add to her first born. Her son Thomas was born in 1880 in the workhouse at Omagh. Her first daughter, Mary, was born the following year on the 19th of May 1882. Matthew was aware of his undertakings as the Parish Register of Births, Marriages and Deaths saw fit to include a red ink annotation beside the child's name: "Illegitima. Pater pensa est Jacobus Maguire".

(This may be the same Joseph Maguire of Tempo riot fame mentioned above). I struggle to understand why the Church needed to record this against the child. And the anguish caused to the young mother?

Interrogations over the identity of the natural father will have been a torturous experience for her. Illegitimacy counted for about 4% of all births in late Victorian Britain. In England, the Parish would provide some benefits to illegitimate children of an unknown father and indeed would hold the father to account if identified. This did not apply in Mary's case. She had already wed a willing surrogate father. My conclusion is that the Roman Catholic church recorded paternity as an insurance device, lining up Maguire to minimise its financial exposure if Sarah and Matthew split up, or if Matthew died. It ignored the enduring emotional torment of a vulnerable young woman in a rural community.

Despite these difficult beginnings, Mary would lead a very productive and interesting life. In 1907, in the same Tempo church where her mother had wed Matthew Symington, Mary married John McLoughlin from Enniskillen. She had met John while they were both in service at Tempo Manor. Together, they would create ten children between 1908- 1925, including George and Kathleen, always known as Dolly. I met Dolly in the early 1980s in Ontario. A very engaging woman and long-term resident of Los Angeles, Dolly had married into the Holywood "set". She was a first-hand witness to my grandfather's IRA days and revealed that Andy had been the most wanted man in Tyrone by the authorities. She will return to our story in due course...

In March 1929, John McLoughlin set sail for New Brunswick. He intended to prepare the way for Mary and the family to follow. And so, it transpired in 1930 aged forty-eight, Mary would take the bold step of emigrating to Canada with her family. She set sail on August 1st, 1930. Her transatlantic voyage would last for one week. She alighted in Montreal before laying permanent roots in Toronto. Like many an Irish mother, she would broaden the Irish diaspora in the desperate hope of creating a better future for her children.

Canada proved a good move for the McLoughlin family. John prospered and had a park named after him in Brampton, Ontario.

Mary wasn't the first sibling to marry. Nor were she and John the first McLoughlin-Symington matrimonial union! Some five years earlier, John's older brother, Thomas, had married Mary's younger sister, Ellen, in Fivemiletown. The name Ellen came from her grandmother, Helen Nunn, who had married William Symington, Matthew's father. Ellen and Thomas McLoughlin also had a very fruitful union, resulting in six girls and three boys. Their marriage certificate claims Ellen's age to be twenty-two when, in fact, she had not turned twenty. The minimum legal age for marriage was twenty-one and common practice recorded twenty-two as a popular age on many marriage certificates of that time. A brother and sister from one family marrying a brother and sister from another was a not uncommon occurrence in rural Ireland, a fact attested to by my own parents. Enshrined in the lyrics of the ballad:

"I have often heard it said By my father and my mother That going to a wedding Is the making of another!"

In a world devoid of coffee shops and where cinema had not been invented, a wedding represented a rare opportunity to socialise with the opposite sex in a happy, celebratory environment. All hands would have scrubbed up and donned their "Sunday best". Unlike Mass, which provided a social opportunity that was time restricted and constrained by notions of religious and Victorian morality, the wedding feast encouraged dancing and condoned some consumption of alcohol. The prevailing Irish mentality condemned alcohol as "the demon drink". Teetotallers, or "pioneers" in the vernacular, commanded more respect and were quick to distinguish themselves with a pin bearing the Sacred Heart worn in the lapel.

The Church held a pivotal and domineering role in society. A sizeable chunk of the weekly routine of the local clergy involved administering "the Pledge". This committed a boozy miscreant (often under severe domestic pressure) to desist from alcohol for a period. One month was the minimum and three months more typical of the offering required to restore matrimonial harmony. Like his older brother James, Andy Symington struggled with drink throughout his life. Such was the spirit of his wife Lizzie that he was regularly on bended knee in the Parochial House. In the sixty-year course of his adult life, he took more pledges than Great Ormond St Hospital! Giving his word was a deadly serious commitment for Andy. As an old man, he cherished his reputation of never having broken a Pledge. I digress.

Peter, Mary and Ellen were the first of ten progenies to depend on Matthew and Sarah for survival. With the children arriving over a seventeen-year period, it will have put an inordinate strain on the physical wellbeing of Sarah and the earning capability of Matthew. Reflecting from the relative prosperity of the twenty-first century, their life was grindingly hard. They experienced many of the social deprivations that accompany abject poverty. Matt could not sustain a livelihood as a cobbler and reverted to casual labour. As late as 1910, the Mid Ulster Mail reported the average weekly wage of agrarian labourers as between six and seven shillings (thirty to thirty-five pence in today's money). A skilled labourer or surfaceman could earn between nine and ten shillings. Both cases included board. Typical rents for a small cottage varied between one shilling and sixpence to one shilling and ninepence. Feeding a large family left little for luxuries like rent and Matt had to move house frequently. Sometimes in search of a lower cost, sometimes to be closer to his work. Also, sadly, because of eviction for non-payment.

"If it wasn't for bad luck, I would have no luck at all!"

A sentiment captured by my uncle Patsy rather more colourfully, after a disastrous day in the bookies: "If it was raining fannies, I 'd get the wife's!"

We can trace Matthews' early moves from the birth certificates of his children. He flitted like a butterfly in a four-mile radius between Tempo and Fivemiletown. This took him to parishes like Cavans where my grandfather was born, Creagh, Coralongford, Brookeborough and Tullyweel. The 1901 Census saw the family resident in Tonnagh-More about three miles to the west of Fintona. Next move they were in Syonfin, two miles due south of Fintona on the road to Fivemiletown. In May 1903, the Strabane Chronicle reported that Mrs Amy McClintock of the Ecclesville Estate won a decree of possession against Matthew Symington. Her bailiff was John Mellon. He had made several unsuccessful attempts to deliver the writ. Never finding Matthew at home, he had fallen foul of his dog, much to the amusement of the court. The heartrending conclusion, though, was eviction. "In no sooner than one week and no later than two months". The stress of eviction coupled with multiple home moves will have put an incalculable strain on the family.

Coalisland emerged as a magnet for urban drift, having industrialised following the early Victorian creation of a canal. As Samuel McKay noted in his excellent history, "Light of Other Days Around Coalisland," the Industrial Revolution was driven by coal, cotton, clay, canals, steam and iron. Remarkably, the small town of Coalisland had all six. It provided non- agricultural jobs that offered a higher wage. A job in earthenware pipes earned a weekly wage of fourteen shillings whereas a clay miner could command the princely sum of fifteen shillings per week. And so, at the turn of the century, Matt sought his fortune in Coalisland and moved the family to Tyrone. He settled in Shambles Lane in Dungannon before moving closer to work at Roan Mills and a house on Mill Row in Brackaville.

He does not feature in the 1901 Census. Sarah is now the head of the house with Matthew, Andrew, Sarah Jane, George and Maggie as dependent children. The Census accredits Matthew, Andrew and Sarah Jane with the ability to read and write and records their ages at ten, eight and six, respectively. George had yet to acquire these skills, although it recorded him as a four-year-old "scholar". A promising debut! The Census collected thirteen pieces of information for each occupant of every household. Column thirteen provides an insight into society at the dawn of the twentieth century. It sought to capture one of five infirmities: Deaf and Dumb; Dumb only; Blind; Imbecile or Idiot; Lunatic.

Column thirteen had no entries against the Symingtons. Deo Gratias! Probably an oversight.

Being a defaulter made a new rental more difficult, and putting the house in Sarah's name was a tactical necessity. His wedding certificate to Sarah Graham in 1881 identified the occupation of the bride's father as a "scutcher". Scutching was a process in manufacturing cotton which separated the impurities from the raw material. The woody stem separated from the fibres of the flax. It was then ready for spinning. The "technology" involved a scutcher thrashing the living daylights out of the flax with a big stick. At his son John's wedding to Mary Anne McKernan in Brackaville in1906, Matthew's occupation had morphed into "scutcher".

"Sure, you couldn't beat it with a big stick!" Matthew may well have proclaimed on his upturn in fortune.

This was a good move for Matthew. His earnings had risen to 12 shillings per week in an article in the Mid Ulster Mail on 28 October 1911. Due to overcrowding in Roan Mills, he was applying for a cottage on the land of John Dooey in Derry. However, he may have been overstating his income, as he also told the court he had ten children. In fact, only five lived with him at that time. His work as a scutcher thus provided a stable and quite rewarding income. He was not to know that his job was already in the cycle of economic decline, on route to extinction. Some four years later, on Tuesday 28 September 1915, the Belfast Newsletter would report on a meeting of flax scutchers at Mr A. Ferguson's Hotel in Cookstown. The issue was a longstanding grievance over pay.

The incoming chair, Mr Thomas McCann, noted that while "the pay for all labour had increased by leaps and bounds, scutchers' wages still dragged behind". About two dozen scutchers from nine local mills attended the meeting. It was unanimously carried that none would return to work until the employers met their demand for 6d per stone. To encourage solidarity, they agreed to blackball any man who returned to work before the mill-owners had increased their offer. The rest would stay out until he was fired. Or deprived of the improved offer, which would be divided amongst the other workers every month. This will have been very stressful for Matthew since so many of his family earned their living in Roan Mills- John, Matt, Andy, Sarah Jane and George. Little wonder that people aged prematurely in such trying times...

Another reason for premature ageing is evident in the Census of 1911 (where Matthew makes a welcome return). In 1908, the Liberal government had introduced the old age pension for people over seventy. This generated a widespread bout of accelerated ageing. In the census decade between 1901 and 1911, older people aged over ten years. Fifteen to twenty years was the typical spread. This may well explain some confusion around Matthew's date of birth, moving from 1856 to 1847. It also marked the genesis of a new industry in Coalisland: Benefits Fraud would endure long after the mills fell silent!

Thomas Symington

Sarah's eldest child, Thomas, was born in the workhouse in Omagh on 15th February, 1880. His father is recorded as "Unknown." A simple birth certificate records his sponsor as "Joseph, Chief Resident Officer of Omagh workhouse." Despite, or perhaps because of, his humble beginnings, Thomas seems to be one who worked hard to improve his lot. His wedding certificate lists his occupation as a dealer.

At the age of twenty-six in 1906, he married Emily Bell in Lisnaskea Registrar's Office. Marrying a Protestant and doing so outside a Catholic church, was a bold step for Thomas and one which will have drawn criticism across his social circle. Their first child, Robert James, was born on August 22, 1907 in Ballymacaffrey near Brookeborough. Socially ostracised but driven by ambition, Thomas decided his family would have a better chance of a future in the US. He set sail later that year from

Liverpool, landing in Boston Harbour. Eighty years later, I made the same trip across the cold and choppy waters of Boston Harbour from Logan airport, destined for a sojourn in the salubrious Boston Harbour Hotel.

Thomas and Emily settled initially in New Hampshire where their daughter Ruth was born in 1909, followed by Edna in 1910. In stark contrast to life in Fermanagh, Thomas and Emma were very mobile and moved home several times in pursuit of improved employment opportunities. They flitted between New Hampshire and Maine before settling in Massachusetts. Thomas adapted to the American way and became a successful machine salesman.

For whatever reason, perhaps social security advantages, he seems to have oscillated between the identities of Graham and Symington. While I am happy to accept the plaudits for an excellent piece of genealogical sleuthing, I must confess to the prompting of a sharp-eyed US federal computer and the tip "Alias: also known as Thomas Symington".

Thomas died in Salem, Massachusetts in 1952. Emily died in 1967 and is buried in Exeter, New Hampshire. To this day, we can find Symingtons in Conshohocken, near Philadelphia.

James Symington

Every large family has a "black sheep", if only comparatively. With the benefit of historical detachment, we can afford some magnanimity, so let us describe my grandfather's older brother James as a "colourful character". James entered the congested Symington household on the 6th of July 1885 as the fourth born and second male. By the turn of the century, he was making his way independently, employed as a farm labourer by John Little, a Presbyterian who farmed with his brothers on lands around Foglish, a townland to the south of Enniskillen. Free accommodation supplemented meagre wages. As was the practice, James lived in relative comfort with John and Rebecca Little, their young daughter Martha and John's widowed mother Margaret.

By the 1911 Census, the lure of Coalisland's bright lights was too much and the country boy had opted for the potential riches of industry and a metropolitan future. Many of his family had already made that migration. Economics were changing. The National Insurance Act of 1911 heralded a landmark step for Worker's Rights and the creation of the Welfare State. Introduced by Lloyd George, it tipped the balance in favour of working in industry. The initial scheme obligated the worker to pay 3d per week; the employers' contribution being set at 4d and the government paying 2d. This entitled the employee to ten shillings per week for up to twenty-six weeks in the event of illness, plus free access to a doctor and free medicine. Other benefits included a maternity grant of thirty shillings.

Thus, by 1911, James was living with his younger brother in Johnny's house in Brackaville. Johnny (commonly known as Jock) had married Mary Annie McCloskey and their first child, Mary Veronica, was a two-year-old toddler. Both Johnny and Mary Annie had jobs in the mills, he as a mill labourer and she as a spinner. James, still a farm labourer, had not penetrated the higher wages of industry. More revealingly, his level of literacy had regressed to "Read Only" whereas in the 1901 Census he could "Read & Write", though tellingly his surname was misspelled. Whether he could read is questionable. Ireland still had the highest rates of illiteracy in the UK. (Over 13% of young males could not read). One of my father's mantras was "a good education is easily carried." The reverse, though, also held true in spades! Illiteracy would have been a punishing disability for James in terms of job opportunities, respect, and self-worth.

In 1911, aged twenty-six, he could not command a job in the mills. It did nothing for his self-respect to know that five of his younger siblings already worked in those industries (John,

Matt, Andy, George, and Sarah Jane). James wallowed in the lowest order of the working classes- the general labourer. (Domestic servant was the equivalent for females). As one observer disparagingly noted, general labourers were "men with no definite trade, ready for anything and good for nothing". His only employment prospects were the farm and seasonal work in the building industry. Derided, isolated, and shorn of ambition, James turned to drink like so many others in a similar plight.

"A good feed of drink" to cite the Tyrone colloquialism bestowed some temporary escape from the hopelessness of his everyday life.

Alcohol can be a pernicious master, and so James' life degenerated as inebriation eroded the last vestiges of self-respect and purpose. His journey was littered with prosecutions and fines for drunkenness. The Tyrone Courier reporting on Dungannon Petty Sessions in August 1909 recorded the case of Constable McManus against James Symington and Patrick Skeffington. To the amusement of the court, the constable said they "were fighting like bears". This resulted in convictions of riotous and indecent behaviour with a fine of 5s 6d. His first recorded offence was in April 1907 when a Constable Bell arrested him for being drunk in Coalisland, culminating in a fine of 3s 6d. (For the benefit of the decimal generations, this amount was articulated as "three & six" and amounted to 17.5 pence) The Mid Ulster Mail of October 1910 published a list from the Stewartstown Assizes with the no frills headline "Coalisland Drunks". James again figured prominently and received a fine of 3s 6d for his efforts. This time, the Court added costs in a sign of growing judicial impatience. January 1911 saw him arrested by Constable Rabbit with a 5-shilling fine.

During this period, James went to Scotland to visit his aunt Ellen. Modern DNA analysis points to the likelihood of him fathering an illegitimate child with a lady called Isabella Kennedy Forsyth. Christened Margaret, the child was adopted soon after her birth in September 1909. She was born in Plean in Stirlingshire, and the likely connection is through the McCaffreys who lived further up the same street- Red Row. James' mother was Sarah Graham, whose younger sister, Ellen, had married into the McCaffreys. Patrick McCaffrey had moved to Scotland with John McLoughlin in 1901, two young men seeking their fortune and Patrick may well have laid his roots in Plean.

Living in Scotland, the McCaffreys became the inadvertent lightning conductor for holiday visitors from the extended family. (Over a century later, my sisters Pamela and Elma would experience the phenomenon from the relatively more enticing venues of San Francisco and Florida, respectively).

James' association with Scotland would continue with his enlistment into the 7th Battalion of the Royal Scottish Fusiliers in 1915. A dissolute decade of dissipation was no preparation for the discipline of army life. And so it proved. He unexpectedly renewed the acquaintance of the Coalisland constabulary when arrested by Constable Lynch on the 25th of September 1915, hiding in his father's house in Red Row, Kettle Lane, Brackaville. Charged with being absent without leave, he spent the night in Coalisland barracks pending a military escort. Acutely short of manpower, the army reunited him with his battalion and on November 17th, 1915, he sailed with his comrades to France. For James, the action would now come thick and fast...

Between enlisting and going absent without leave, James was fortunate to avoid the grisly fate that befell many of his colleagues in the 7th Battalion. On May 22nd, 1915, A and D Companies (i.e., half of the battalion) were entrained on a journey from Larbert in Stirlingshire to Liverpool. As the train approached Quintinshill near Gretna, the worst rail disaster in British railway history was about to unfold. At 6.48, a goods train travelling north wanted to allow the London Glasgow Express to overtake. Unable to move into either of the two railway sidings at Quintinshill which were occupied by other freight vehicles, the goods train parked up momentarily on the southbound line. At 6.49am, the southbound troop carrier hit the stationery goods train head on, derailing and scattering debris everywhere. About ten seconds later, the high-speed Glasgow Express ploughed into the conflagration.

The impact on the 7th Battalion and its home base of Leith was devastating. Two hundred and sixteen men dead or missing, yielding only eighty-three identifiable bodies. A further two hundred and eighteen injured. Only sixty-two were unscathed. It was a complete disaster, but it may well be that the resultant manpower shortages obliged the army to take a lenient view of James' abscondment.

Returned to his battalion, James was wounded on 12th April in the run up to Easter 1916 and the notorious gas attacks at Hulluch, where the Royal Scots defended the Kink position. A German deserter had forewarned the impending gas attack, which was reinforced by aerial photographs showing the build-up of gas inventory. It was definitively confirmed by a mass exodus of rats into No Man's Land to escape from leaking cylinders. These signs being ignored, the gas attacks brought the scything ruthlessness of the Grim Reaper to the men of the 16th

Division. Father Willie Doyle, chaplain to the Dublin Fusiliers, described the horror in front of his eyes the following day:

"There they lay, scores of them in the bottom of the trench, in every conceivable posture of human agony; the clothes torn off their bodies in a vain effort to breathe."

British High Command, rarely missing an opportunity to disgrace itself, initially blamed the high death count on "bad gas discipline" alleging that the men had been careless in fitting their masks. However, they soon had to retract and admit that the gas helmets provided had offered little protection, particularly as Father Doyle had seen many dead bodies with masks properly fitted. To save face, the official history (Military Operations France & Belgium 1916 Volume 1) was re-written to project a more acceptable falsehood. "The helmets in question had not been properly impregnated with chemicals". As usual, somebody (else) had to pay.

James Symington's 7th battalion incurred heavy losses that would see them amalgamate with the 6th in May 1916. Recovered from his wounds, he returned to active service, but military life was not for him. His medal card records him as a deserter on January 12th, 1917. From this point, he becomes the Edwin Drood of the Symington brood. A man of mystery.

Three hundred and forty-six soldiers were executed by firing squad in World War One, including two hundred and sixty-six guilty of desertion. It was the most serious crime for a soldier, ahead of cowardice and mutiny. The average length of trial in the field was nine minutes. Nine minutes! Usually conducted by a junior officer and with little or no medical input. As the war wore on and manpower became scarce, many death sentences were commuted to ten years of penal servitude, to be served on completion of the war. The name of James Symington does not appear in the listings of executed soldiers. Nor have I uncovered it in the Court Martial Registers. There a record of a James Symington found guilty of desertion on October 15th, 1917. A private in the Australian Imperial Force (AIF), he is a different man. Research shows he was born in New South Wales and enlisted on 26th April, 1916 at the sports ground in NSW.

Desertion was quite widespread and became more popular as the War wore on, casualties mounted, and self-preservation replaced chivalrous inanity in the psyche of the reasonable man. Some postcards of the time show desertion had become culturally acceptable. The introduction of conscription in March 1916 stimulated the practice on the Home Front, where it has been estimated that over 57,000 men did not answer their call-up papers. Many men returned to their homes to be harboured. Remote rural areas were quite popular in this pursuit with the village of Cowling near Skipton earning the mantle of "Deserters Village", a dishonour bequeathed by the Yorkshire Post. Remote and peppered with huts concealed in the moors for the grouse season, Cowling became the "Des Res" to see out the war in peace. Care was still advisable though, as the local police could earn a bonus for each deserter apprehended. No doubt Constable Lynch will have been quite pleased to feel the collar of James Symington once again!

James suffered the same fate as Ivor Gurney (see chapter four) who, having been gassed and shellshocked, spent the last fifteen years of his life incarcerated in a mental institution. James was more fortunate. He had a sterling sister, Sarah Jane Morris, who welcomed him to her home in Motherwell. He lived with her until his death in 1960. He never married.

Matthew Symington

Named after his father, Matthew was the pivot in an eponymous trilogy where his dad was differentiated as "Old Matt" and his nephew became "Young Matt". Chronologically the closest brother to Andy, Matthew never strayed far from his Brackaville roots and spent his life working in the Roan Spinning Mill.

Heavier set than my grandfather, he proved a fine Gaelic footballer and like myself, he represented both Brackaville and Coalisland at different stages of his football career. Unlike myself, he played for the Tyrone senior team, featuring in one of the first inter-county games against Cavan.

Matt married another mill worker, Alice Devlin, in Stewartstown chapel in October 1913. She bore him a son, James Charles, affectionately known as "Jim Charlie" in January 1915. Jim Charlie inherited his father's love of football and was a respected goalkeeper. Sadly, he caught tuberculosis (still a killer disease in those days) and died a young man.

Matt and Alice had no more children. He was loyal to his work at the mill, eventually reaching management and living in a comparatively large house (compared with the houses on Mill Row) adjacent to the factory itself. He lived there with Alice and her sister long after the factory closed. When the factory houses were condemned in the 1960s, he packed his bags and emigrated to Irwins Row, a distance of some 400 yards. I was fond of Matt and often visited him in Irwins Row where we would sit by a small fire as he told me stories about football. He liked a drink, but his mobility was impaired, which caused him to use a walking stick, moving ever so slowly with small, shuffling steps. This created opportunities for the author, fetching bottles of stout from Crilly's. It was a lucrative enterprise, often rewarded with a tanner and sometimes a shilling if I managed to alight on Pension Day.

I left Brackaville in September 1973 to read Economics at Hull. I never saw Matt again. God bless him.

Sarah Jane

Sarah was born during her father's fleeting residence at Brookeborough in January, 1895. Her older sister, Mary, was present at the birth and stood as her godparent.

After a stint in the mill, work dried up for women after the war and she emigrated to Motherwell in Scotland, leveraging the McCaffrey connection. Sarah seems to have been independent and energetic. She quickly established her own home in Russell Place, before moving to Plean Street.

She married Peter Morris in the Roman Catholic church in Motherwell on April 12th, 1920. They had one son, also Peter, who I met many years ago when he visited Derryvale Road on holiday. Sarah seems to have been the family anchor for the Symingtons. Her house was the "go to" place in time of trouble. She was there for her younger sister Margaret when she became pregnant. When my grandfather was forced into exile after the Irish Civil War in 1923, he spent two years with Sarah in Motherwell. See Volume Two of Andy's story. She also cared for her rakish brother James when he returned from the war. A broken man, suffering from the long-term effects of being gassed, Sarah provided for him until his death in 1960.

Sarah died in East Kilbride in 1974. She was a remarkable woman, a standout sibling.

George Symington

My grandfather's youngest brother, George, was born in Maguiresbridge, Fermanagh, on April 14th, 1897. In the 1911 census, he was in employment as a mill worker at the tender age of fourteen. This was typical of the time: records in Belfast showed that only one child in sixty transitioned from National school (i.e. primary) to secondary school. In 1911 in Belfast, some 15,000 children did not have a school. Of those who did, absenteeism was rife. Many children between the ages of 10-14 would alternate their days between school and the linen mills where they could earn a few shillings to supplement a hard-pressed family budget.

On May 14th, 1915, George took the train to Derry and enlisted in the army. It was a bold initiative for an eighteen-year-old who stood five feet four and one quarter and who weighed in at one hundred and four pounds (less than seven and a half stones or 43 kilos, if you prefer new money). Not the sort of physical specimen to worry the Kaiser unduly, yet I sense a powerful spirit. One which reappeared a generation later in my uncle Patsy, another small man with a huge personality and a feistiness that commanded respect. Whether it was due to playing outside left for Coalisland Celtic in his youth is unclear, but Patsy was a committed left winger all his life. His appetite for hard work was distinguishing and matched that of his legendary older brother, Aloysius (Wishy).

One of Patsy's predecessors on the wing for Coalisland Celtic is worth a mention. John McNally was a gifted footballer but an exceptionally small man at under 5 feet. He earned the nickname "Montana" when he and some of his mates crowded around a wireless in 1937 to listen to a fight between Pat Palmer of London and Small Montana, the diminutive US featherweight champion. By all accounts, it was a terrific fight, and the excitement spilled over to the listeners in Derryvale Road, causing John McNally to trade blows with a larger opponent. "Go on small

Montana" roared a supporter, coining a moniker that would stick like glue for 50 years. It also elevated him into celebrity's super elite- those known by one name only- Mandela, Madonna, Mozart, Montana! In one eye-catching performance for Celtic at the Legion Park, he drew praise from a visiting opposition supporter: "That lad on the wing is a great prospect." Montana was 35 at the time!

Returning to Patsy's uncle, George Symington volunteered for the Royal Inniskilling Fusiliers, doubtless hoping to be reunited with some of his Fermanagh school chums. He probably paid little attention to the recruiting sergeant when he read question sixteen, which advised that although they would make every effort to post him to his preferred regiment, he could, in fact be posted to any regiment in the Corps... George duly took up a post in the Northumberland Fusiliers. He signed up for seven years in the Colours and five in the Reserve. Question seventeen on George's Attestation form also provides insight into the British Army's lack of preparedness for the horrific realities of trench warfare. It advised the recruit that although he was enlisting for a dismounted corps, he was "liable to be trained and employed in such mounted duties as may be required".

George will have bemoaned his luck on his assignment to the "Geordie brigade" but hindsight shows good timing can offset bad luck. Two of his namesakes from the Tempo area, George and Robert Symington successfully enrolled in the Royal Inniskilling Fusiliers. Neither would return. George died at the Somme, Robert at Arras.

Recalled from the Front, George spent Christmas 1916 in a hospital in Birmingham. For forty-one long days, he was treated for dysentery in the Southern General on Dudley Road. Poor sanitation and contaminated water created the ideal conditions for dysentery. 1916 was one of the coldest winters ever and records show the temperature at -20 celsius or lower for six consecutive weeks.

There was one story of the soldiers breaking the ice on an adjacent shell hole to use as drinking water, which was always in short supply. This continued for several days until the level of ice receded to reveal a pair of boots... on closer inspection, the boots contained feet which were attached to a body. On the other hand, one Tommy had reason to bless the icy conditions when a German shell landed within a yard of him, only to bounce off the hard ground and explode harmlessly, high in the air!

George returned to the front for a further period of active service but was discharged from the army on Oct 6th, 1917. This transpired to be a couple of months after the discharge of his older brother, Andrew. The army doctors considered him to be 40% disabled through a condition then known as "Disordered Action of the Heart" (DAH). Commonly referred to among the medical profession as "Soldier's Heart", it only received serious medical attention and research towards the end of World War One. For simplicity, let us differentiate DAH from Shellshock by saying that the former is physical and the latter mental, though in fact, both carry some common symptoms, such as anxiety and depression. In those pre-PTSD days, medicine knew little about the effects of combat on neurology. Some four hundred and sixty-two soldiers were discharged because of shellshock and admitted to the National Hospital for the Paralysed and Epileptic at Queen Square in London. Britain's ugly class distinction was evident in both the hospital and treatment of shellshock: officers like Siegfried Sassoon and Wilfred Owen were treated at Craiglockhart hospital in Edinburgh.

George's discharge was honourable and a note on his record confirms his character as "very good".

With a (probably understated) forty per cent disability and a post-war economy on its knees through protectionism (the wisdom of Keynes General Theory would not emerge for another fifteen years), George's prospects for employment would have been bleak in the extreme. However, he stuck to his guns and eventually, in March 1920, he was awarded an army pension of sixteen shillings per week. Government cost-cutting reduced it in August 1921 to a thirty per cent disability with a lower commensurate payment of twelve shillings per week. This would prove to be George's staple income until 1924 and possibly up to 1932, the point at which the handwritten entries on his pension card ceased. George married Annie McCloskey and together they would have a daughter, May, and two sons, Hugh and Kevin. He spent the rest of his days in Coalisland and established himself as a popular barber in the town from premises on Seagoe Terrace. Sadly, he would die early, at the age of forty-three.

Margaret

The youngest of my grandfather's siblings was born in December 1899 and worked in Roan Mill after leaving school.

Falling pregnant in Coalisland, she moved to stay with her sister Sarah Jane in Scotland. Her son William was born on January 10th 1921 in 81, Russell Place, Motherwell.

Later that year, on July 4th, Margaret married Robert Nelson in Glasgow. Robert was a twenty-year-old private in the 2nd Battalion of the Gordon

Highlanders, stationed at Maryhill Barracks. The wedding certificate was witnessed by her sister Sarah and bore her address: 81 Park Street, Motherwell.

Margaret and Robert had a son together, Matthew (named after Margaret's father.) After Robert's discharge from the army, they settled in Dumfries. Following Robert's death in 1975, Margaret moved to Halifax in West Yorkshire to be closer to her son. She died in 1987. Sadly, I never knew she was there. I visited Halifax many times in the early 1980s when the builders' merchant, C Bancroft, was my customer. I drove a 3.0ltr gold Capri at the time, which had a sunroof- I feel sure Margaret would have been impressed!

3   THE SOMME

The First Battle of the Somme started on July 1st, 1916. It lasted until November 18th. An orgy of slaughter without parallel. It was a joint French-British initiative, conceived by Joffre and Haig at the Allied conference in Chantilly in late 1915. Although the German defences were known to be exceptionally strong on the Somme, Haig displayed his persistent disregard for the lives of common soldiers and set three towering objectives:

    1. Overrun the German front line trenches.

    2. Take the heavily fortified second line trenches known as the "Schwaben Redoubt".

    3. Advance up the hill and capture enemy trenches on the Grandcourt- Serre Ridge.

To facilitate these objectives, they planned a five- day artillery bombardment. It has been estimated that 1.75 million shells were fired during that bombardment. Over 225,000 shells were fired during the last hour of the barrage. In fact, during that week, the British fired more shells than in the first twelve months of the war. Many of them were duds as our American cousins sacrificed quality control in pursuit of a fast buck. (It is believed that more than one in four failed to detonate.) The First World War might equally be termed the "first Industrial world war," as seen from the unprecedented level of shelling over the four years. Military historians estimated that the combatants exchanged 700 million munitions. Even if only 10% of those failed to explode, it litters the French and Belgian countryside with around 70 million unexploded bombs! As a minimum. Every year since 1918, some people have been killed by the detonation of WW1 shells. The total number of deaths since the war is estimated at over 900.

There remain tracts of land closed to humans. The French government defined a "Zone Rouge" where humans are forbidden to access. It takes the form of a fractured crescent, stretching from Lille to Nancy, taking in Verdun, Cambrai and Somme towns, some of which have never been inhabited since. Even after over one hundred years of cleaning up by the Deminage (mine clearance and bomb disposal team), the Zone Rouge still amounts to some 120 square kilometres of land (an area bigger than Paris). Stark signs explain: "Impossible to clean. Human Life impossible." The issue is partly unexploded munitions, but it is also the residue of chemical warfare, which both sides deployed. Phosgene, chlorine and mustard gasses have seeped into the charred and churned ground, causing massive contamination. Tests conducted in the last ten years have revealed arsenic levels at ten thousand times the norm. Some experts have estimated that it could take 700 years to fully clear the "Red Zone."

Back to the action. On X-Y night, the assaulting troops would move into their forward trenches. "Zero hour" was set at 7.30 a.m. next morning. As was customary, no-one stated the date of an offensive. Regimental records reveal June 27th as the original X-Y night.

Planning such an attack exercised complex logistics. They had to co-ordinate artillery, infantry, engineers, air and medical services, signals, gas, trench mortar batteries and all supply services including stores and accessories. The build-up ramped from June 7th. Heightening the nervous anticipation of those going "over the top". Preparation included some familiarisation/practice, and the First Battalion visited the Louvencourt training ground near Vauchelles-les-Authie on June 22nd. There, they spent three days rehearsing attacks on dummy trenches configured to portray their objectives. On the torrential night of June 27th, the Faughs moved into tents at Bertrancourt. Tension mounted. The anticipation of battle. The sickening fear of imminent death. All repressed in a mask of communal joviality.

God knows the impact on nerves when bad weather forced a delay of 48 hours, postponing Zero day to July 1st. This created the conditions for unprecedented bloodshed in the Belfast Unionist community. The Faughs assumed responsibility for 375 yards of the front. At 9pm on June 30th, they marched forward into their Assembly trenches at Sunken Road, arriving at 12.35 a.m. Although there was heavy shelling in the vicinity, they reached the position without casualties. So far, so good. In contrast to the preceding days, the sun rose on July 1st, introducing a beautiful morning.

The Allied advance was spearheaded by the 36th Ulster Regiment, part of the 11th Brigade. Stationed in Thiepval Wood, they knew acutely July 1st was the anniversary of the Battle of the Boyne. At Zero hour, whistles sounded, and they went over the top. Each man carried around 66lbs of supplies or, on average, half their body weight. Supplies included a shovel, barbed wire and signalling equipment. Driven by the feats of their ancestors and a perceived call of Destiny, the Ulstermen fought ferociously. They succeeded in taking both the first and second line of German trenches.

Across the battlefront, though, other units in the 11th Brigade had less success. The artillery barrage had not cut the barbed wire in front of the German trenches, nor had made any impact on deep German dugouts. The devastating result was Tommies bunching up around a few openings in the wire and walking into a hail of concentrated machine gun fire. Part of the German line formed a salient, which was like a promontory jutting out into No Mans Land. This feature provided a huge strategic advantage as the Germans could fire diagonally on both sides, inflicting much heavier casualties than shooting at a line of soldiers head-on.

The speed of the 36th Ulsters advance had isolated them. Their success exposed them to fire from both flanks. A turkey shoot ensued. It cost the Ulsters two thousand dead and some five thousand wounded. The 1st day of the Somme was the darkest day in British Military history. Fifty-seven thousand casualties, including over nineteen thousand fatalities in an unprecedented holocaust of young men.

The Faugh-A-Ballaghs, meanwhile, could thank Providence they had emerged relatively unscathed from Haig's plan. As part of the 11th Division, their mission was to overtake the 10th Division after the latter had achieved the first two objectives and lead the assault on the third target by taking Beaucourt-sur-Ancre. Their participation being thus much reduced, losses only amounted to 15 killed and 90 wounded. Their colleagues in the 9th Battalion of the Royal Irish Fusiliers were less fortunate. They were dispatched in support of the Ulstermen and suffered heavy losses. A chilling note in the regimental diary states that men of A and B companies made it beyond the enemy first line- "none returned."

    Private 24168: Andy Symington spent the day in a forward trench awaiting the "three white lights" signal to go over the top. Luckily for him, it never came. Three white lights were the signal meaning "we have reached objectives." A single white light meant "held up by wire". So many single white lights flashing in the early confusion looked like multiples. Communication amidst the chaos will have been challenging in the extreme. Eventually, at 10.35 a.m. a telephone message from HQ advised the 10th Brigade to forego the planned attack until further orders. The Regimental Diary records this message was received as the leading platoons had advanced from the assembly trenches "in battle formation". They were literally seconds from going over the top. Seconds from becoming another ingredient in the wok of futile sacrifice. The First Battalion of the Royal Irish Fusiliers remained stationary in a line between

Mountjoy and Tenderloin trenches. On orders. The relief will have been palpable.

The entire infantry attack had lasted less than three hours, though most of the casualties occurred within the first fifteen minutes. Many were killed within twenty yards of leaving their trench, as they rose to face a withering hail of machine gun fire. So much for the leadership's exhortation "Bapaume by nightfall, Berlin by Christmas." Those who managed to progress further, found the barbed wire largely intact. Often it looked like an artillery dump, where unexploded shrapnel shells (due to poor fuses) lay beside the wire they were designed to obliterate.

I can't imagine the air of melancholy and depression that descended over the Somme on July 2 when the killing paused and both sides drew breath to consider what had happened. And what they had created. The visual will have far exceeded Dante's inferno with bodies everywhere in a mangle of broken trenches, severed limbs and gorging rats. Add the odour of rotting flesh peppered with the smell of excrement from bowel movements that accompany sudden death. Exhausted Tommies and Bosch staring in mute witness to the indignity of Death.

Most torturous of all- the sound! The sounds of wailing wounded drifting in from No Man's Land. Too dangerous to reach them after the frenzy, they left them to lie, beg and cry. Many called for their mothers as their life ebbed into the shellholes, and they made the lonely transition from son to statistic. Others would scream in agony. Such was the aggregation of noises, like a packed football stadium, it was impossible to pick out individual sounds as the cacophony synthesised into a single unearthly whine. An eerie, unsettling sound, persisting before dwindling into the chalk of the Somme and the silence of Eternity.

Survivors busied themselves with burying the dead (those they could reach) and restoring dignity like the house-proud clean up after dinner. Clearing the debris of battle and repairing the structure of trenches brought welcome monotony. It left less room for reflection on the carnage that enveloped them. They returned to their activities mechanically and didn't have time to grieve.

They knew their future dictated more of the same.

There followed four days of nothingness. Brit and German, Tommy and Fritz, sat amid the detritus of death in the open cemetery that was the Somme valley. The awful stench of decomposing flesh was a shared torment. Sun and rain had blackened the bodies. In darkness and hopeless desolation, the indomitable greatness of the human spirit can emerge, as indeed it did on the afternoon of July 5th.

The British raised a large Red Cross flag over the parapet of their frontline trench. The bearer remained hidden. After a couple of minutes, no shots being fired, two doctors climbed gingerly out of the trench. One of them was Lieutenant Colonel Fitzpatrick, RAMC. The Germans held their fire as the two advanced across No Man's Land. Reciprocation was almost immediate. A German officer wearing a Red Cross brassard and carrying an impromptu white flag tied to a walking stick, clambered over the parapet. He met his enemies halfway. They exchanged a formal salute, and other medics joined both sides. They spent the afternoon with the Germans carrying wounded Tommy survivors who had fallen close to their lines back over to the British. The British medics then ferried them across the British lines for much needed medical support. No word was spoken in an act of chivalry both heart-warming and rare. After several hours, the two officers reconvened in the middle, saluted, and walked away. Not one soldier fired a shot. By 11 p.m. that same evening, both artilleries had resumed their grotesque symphony...

The rhythm of trench warfare revolved around a six-day cycle. The Faughs would be relieved at the front often by the Seaforth Highlanders before spending six-day blocks on rest & recuperation, training, drilling, and occasional organised sports days. Sometimes they endured stirring speeches in the clipped tones of some aristocratic incompetent intoning about what a good job they were doing and how proud he was to be their commanding officer. Buttered up, they would return to the front for six days and relieve the Seaforths.

On the 8th of July, the "aristocratic incompetent" visiting the men was the Corps Commander himself! (To contextualise military structures in order of importance (size): Army; Corps; Division; Brigade; Regiment, Battalion, Company, Platoon). Lieutenant General Sir Aylmer Hunter- Weston "made a stirring speech" in which he explained the enemy had expected the attack and had concentrated their forces against the Corps. However, the vigorous attacks of the V111 Corps had greatly assisted the attacks made further south… I very much doubt whether this thinly veiled attempt at vindication of Top-Brass Strategy will have washed with my grandfather and his comrades. Siegfried Sassoon's short poem "The General" better reflected the feelings of the common soldier:

"Good-morning, good-morning! the General said When we met him last week on our way to the line. Now the soldiers he smiled at are most of 'em dead, And we're cursing his staff for incompetent swine. "He's a cheery old card," grunted Harry to Jack As they slogged up to Arras with rifle and pack. But he did for them both by his plan of attack."

With Gallipoli and the Somme on his c.v., Hunter-Weston earned the reputation as "one of the most brutal and incompetent commanders of the First World War." Even Haig called him a "rank amateur" (proof if needed that the source of the insult can deepen the wound!) Like Haig, Hunter-Weston believed that if the objective was worth gaining, casualties did not matter. This earned them, and their ilk, the nickname "Thrusters." Like Haig, he was a cavalry man clinging to an anachronistic model from the Boer War. As my grandfather listened to his false thanks (a triumph of insincerity and bluster), he would not have known that the blood on this General's hands cut well beyond arrogance and incompetence.

Hunter-Weston himself had ordered the detonation of the forty-thousand-pound bomb the Royal Engineers had lain under the Hawthorn Ridge Redoubt, a heavily fortified position west of Beaumont Hamel. He insisted on detonating it at seven twenty a.m., a full ten minutes before the British advance. This time lag allowed the Germans to man the craters before the British had crossed No Man's Land. Elsewhere on the front, they detonated the mines between 7.28 and 7.30am, to avoid this precise outcome.

Having told the infantry they could walk over the German lines with little resistance because of the bombardment, history shows he had received detailed reports on June 30 that their defensive barbed wire remained intact. He also received intelligence from a Royal Dublin Fusiliers scouting party that the German trenches were exceptionally deep (over sixty feet). He knew they were therefore better prepared to withstand bombardment. Finally, in this section of the attack, the Germans occupied the high ground unlike conditions further south. Yet Hunter-Weston and Haig insisted on launching the attack over a wide front.

The text of Hunter-Weston's speech that day is recorded in the Regimental Diary. Ignoring the litany of mistakes he had made, he adopted a completely different stance to his position of two weeks earlier: "We had the most difficult part of the line to attack" (True, but the topography had been the same for millennia).

"The Germans had fortified it with great skill for many months and had their best troops there and a formidable collection of artillery and machine guns" (Most if not all, of which he knew beforehand).

The statistics provide a chilling "res ipse loquitur": V111 Corps lost 14,581 men that day or 75% of the highest daily losses the British Army had ever experienced. Of the three corps involved in the attack, "only the V111 Corps was completely unsuccessful" (Wilson, 2005)

These numbers cover day one. The Somme would grind on for another four months. A sustained exercise in futility and senseless sacrifice. The bloodiest battle in the history of mankind, ultimately almost one million men perished, friend and foe. With numbers so enormous, a statistical tsunami, it is near impossible to remember that each one of these was a mother's son. Each had a story to tell. They had ambitions, talent and hopes. Each lost to a world that would never know the extent of its loss. In acknowledgement of the talent wasted, of those who would have claimed their place in history had they been allowed to live, I exhibit Tom Kettle. Few will have heard of him. That is the point.

Lieutenant Tom Kettle of the Royal Dublin Fusiliers was thirty-six years old when he lost his life at the Somme on September 9th, 1916. He fell during the 16th Irish Division's attack on Ginchy.

A leading Nationalist of his day, he became a Member of Parliament for East Tyrone (my grandfather's constituency) after the 1906

General Election. The margin of victory was one of the narrowest in parliamentary history- eighteen votes. The first of two elections in 1910 re-elected him. He did not contest the second one.

Educated at University College Dublin where he befriended Padraig Pearse and James Joyce, he possessed a prodigious intellect. By 1908, aged twenty-eight, he was professor of National Economics at UCD. He saw the future of Ireland as being European rather than British. This vision was unique and well ahead of his time. Fluent in French and German, he joined the Irish Volunteers in 1913. He was in Belgium buying arms for the Volunteers in August 1914. A first-hand witness to the ferocity of the German invasion, he also noted the corresponding inability of the weaker Belgian Military to resist.

Writing for the Daily News, he was unequivocal in his thoughts:

"It is impossible not to be with Belgium in this struggle. It is impossible any longer to be passive. Germany has thrown down a well-considered challenge to all the deepest forces of our civilisation. War is hell, but it is only a hell of suffering, not a hell of dishonour. And through it, over its flaming coals, Justice must walk, were it on bare feet."

On his return to Dublin, it was easy for him to support Redmond's call for Nationalists to enlist.

It is obvious his decision to enlist was no tactic on the road to Home Rule, but borne of the highest moral principles in support of the weak against the bully. In a small country like Belgium, he saw strong parallels with Ireland. His vision for a thriving Ireland in a peaceful Europe was on the line. He threw himself energetically into the enlistment versus neutrality debate. For him, it was not about supporting England. It was about stopping Germany.

"We are fighting for Ireland. We have agreed to lay all political questions under a moratorium. Prussianism is the end of small nations and Ireland must be defended on the Continent."

Taking his own medicine, he went to the front in 1916. He returned to Dublin to recuperate from illness just before Easter...

"All changed. Changed utterly."

Those words of William Butler Yeats will have resonated like an earthquake with Tom Kettle. The British handling of the Rising's aftermath had stranded Kettle on the wrong side of the narrative. He instantly appreciated that his friend Padraig Pearse would spend eternity as a martyred hero. Whereas Irishmen would see him as a "bloody British officer."

Back at the Somme near Hulluch, the Germans had launched a major offensive behind a bombardment of chlorine gas. His fellow Irishmen in the 16th Division bore the brunt of the losses, with five hundred and thirty-two of them losing their lives. In the contemporaneous Easter Rising in Ireland, "only" four hundred and eighty-eight died. The pen of history would record the latter as heroes, while condemning the former as fools. I see them as neighbours on the spectrum of futility. It had created a schism. A schism that tormented Irish culture for a century.

Knowing that history would condemn him as one of the "fools" and conscious of his own mortality, Lieutenant Kettle stuck to his principles. He returned to the Somme horrors to defend small nations and his European ideal. Unlike many young comrades, Kettle was lucky to be a father. It was to his three-year-old daughter that he wrote his last poem, a few days before his death.

To My Daughter Betty, The Gift of God
"In wiser days, my darling rosebud, blown
To beauty proud as was your mother's prime,
In that desired, delayed, incredible time,
You'll ask why I abandoned you, my own,
And the dear heart that was your baby throne,
To dice with death. And oh! they'll give you rhyme And reason: some will call the thing sublime,
And some decry it in a knowing tone.
So here, while the mad guns curse overhead,

And tired men sigh with mud for couch and floor,
Know that we fools, now with the foolish dead,
Died not for flag, nor King, nor Emperor –
But for a dream, born in a herdsman's shed,
And for the secret Scripture of the poor."

This is a beautiful piece. The political grandmaster playing the game that was not moves but years ahead! He was protecting his daughter from the future pain of criticism of her dead father. He was rendering ignorant those claiming that he was a fool or just a British officer. In dark days and times of vulnerability, Betty could read these words, reassured that he was no fool. She knew the inside story. Her dad was an idealist who had fought to create a fairer world. That he could express such tenderness while surrounded by horror is a towering monument to his dignity and love.

Kettle had foreseen the schism and knew it would cost him his place in history. George Russell's poem, "To the Memory of Some I Knew Who Are Dead and Who Loved Ireland", represented an early but vain attempt to commemorate the dead of both World War One and the Rising:

"You proved by death as true as they,
In mightier conflicts played your part,

Equal your sacrifice may weigh,
Dear Kettle, of the generous heart . . ."

Had he survived, Thomas Kettle's brain would have left a deeper mark on Irish history of the twentieth century. His predicted comparison with his friend Padraig Pearse was perceptive as ever. Pearse, whose body was dissolved in quicklime by the British, is remembered in Arbour Hill behind the National Museum of Ireland and commemorated in the pantheon of martyrs and greats in Glasnevin cemetery. Kettle will spend eternity exiled in an unknown grave in a foreign land. Some tokens to his memory persist, including a bust in St Stephens Green. The Thomas Kettle Award is a prestigious life membership bestowed by the UCD Economics Society. Kettle Lane in Coalisland commemorates his work as the MP for East Tyrone. It is another link with my grandfather who lived there with his father Matthew for several years.

We will consider British Army Military Strategy in a subsequent chapter.

First, we must focus on my grandfather's life in the trenches.

4   LIFE IN THE TRENCHES

Trench warfare was a curiosum. It had never been seen before 1914. After 1918, it would never be seen again. Yet its short four-year life span would generate the most military casualties in the entire history of human conflict. Not to be confused with "digging in", a common practice in the American Civil War and subsequent hostilities, trench warfare defined a continuous line of trenches from the North Sea to the Swiss border. A face off spanning over four hundred miles with no possibility of circumvention. The only way was forward. Head on. Above, across, and beneath ground. All tactics and strategies converging into a single objective: how to punch a hole in a heavily defended line?

By the time Private Andrew Symington entered the fray, the Great War had already been waging for almost two years, and trench warfare had become an established reality. The rhythm, heartbeat, and processes existed and were accepted. Despite the unprecedented carnage of 1914 and 1915 that forced the introduction of conscription in January 1916 in the UK (but not in Ireland), the replacement of idealists with conscripts made little difference. They just carried on. No wide-scale rebellion. Continuity was ensured through recognition of the high price that had already been paid. Those sacrifices must not be in vain. The poem "In Flanders Fields" was a typical clarion call. Written by the Canadian surgeon John McCrae and first published in December 1915:

"In Flanders fields the poppies blow
Between our crosses row on row
That mark our place; and in the sky
The larks, still bravely singing, fly
Scarce heard amid the guns below.
We are the Dead. Short days ago,
We lived, felt dawn, saw sunset glow,
Loved and were loved, and now we lie In Flanders fields.
Take up our quarrel with the foe;
To you from failing hands we throw
The torch; be yours to hold it high.
If ye break faith with us, who die
We shall not sleep, though poppies grow In Flanders fields."

Although my grandfather was a volunteer and not a conscript, I very much doubt whether the distinction will have gained him any kudos, particularly in an Irish regiment where conscription did not apply. The prevailing sentiment among the troops was one of resolute acceptance. There was camaraderie based on a shared Fate, underwritten by a mutually caring generosity. Sharing everything down to your last butt was the way of life when death was close. No matter how bad it got, there was a compulsion to "soldier on". They had already spilled too much blood.

The atmosphere in the trenches was unique. Such a huge number of men, friend and foe, congested into a highly condensed space, yet everyone out of sight. To reveal oneself meant instant death. In the absence of an "over the top" attack, which often occurred at dawn, life in the trench during daylight hours was quite mundane. Apart from the occasional whine of a sniper's pot-shot, things were usually quiet, allowing soldiers to eat, catch up on sleep, update diaries and write letters to loved ones at home. They devoted much time to the repairing of the trench after shelling.

In contrast to German trenches which were engineered to the finest Teutonic principles, British trenches were much more rickety affairs, probably architected by Piecemeal and Patchy, Bodgers to His Majesty. This was partly because the Germans were keen to hold on to the territorial gains they had made, the onus resting with the Allies to oust them. My grandfather's battalion prided themselves on handing over the trenches in good order, although this was not always possible, as it depended on the severity of the fighting and the timing of the typical six-day relief cycle.

The weather was also a factor. The sunny, first day at the Somme was followed later that week by heavy rainfall and flooding, which turned the trenches into an even sorrier mess by the time the Seaforths relieved the First Battalion on July 7th. As well as tidying up the detritus of battle, maintenance sometimes would involve patiently deepening the trench, digging away the chalk to a level which would enable men to at least stand upright while remaining under cover. Removing the need to crouch in certain sections of the line made things more bearable and probably spared the lives of some "forgetful" or absent minded. That said, the depth of the trench was constrained by the physical terrain of the landscape. Much of the battlefield was above a naturally high-water table. This often restricted the depth of the trench to less than five feet. Sandbags were then placed on top to raise the level beyond the vision of the ever-present snipers.

Best practice soon dictated that trenches be constructed with twists and turns every ten yards or so. This prevented a bomb blast from going all the way along a trench and maximising casualties. Narrow and cloistered to reduce the possibility of direct hits, it was almost impossible to manoeuvre stretchers along the trench. The very famous picture of a wounded colleague being carried on the back of a Lancastrian sergeant, was a practical necessity if the wounded were to reach a casualty station.

"Bearable" though is a euphemism for unbelievably awful. Often up to their thighs in mud (or indeed icy water in winter), constantly hungry, exhausted, subjected to unwavering rigid discipline, proximity to rats and always under the constant threat of death. As someone with a strong aversion to rats, sharing a trench with Rattus Norvegicus (the brown rat which thrived in the trenches) would have been an extra Purgatory if one were needed. Tom Kettle records trying to sleep while rats "scurry across your blankets and your face". Such was everyday life in what Kettle described as "Ratavia". Candlelit rat shooting sessions at least provided a competitive distraction for many of the subalterns. ("Subaltern" referred to second lieutenants, the lowest level of officer, invariably young members of the privileged classes, often straight out of university or public school.) Variations included the use of a bayonet as one second lieutenant explained: "A great trick with these rats is to put a bit of cheese on the bayonet and rest it on the parapet and when the rat starts nibbling pull the trigger. Result: no rat!"

Personal hygiene involved getting rid of the lice which prevailed in their hair and inside their shirts. Pediculus Vestmentii was a 4mm-long body louse which would lay daily batches of five eggs in the seams of clothing. On hatching, they would suck the blood of their host, causing irritation. The natural reaction to scratch would open the wound, making it susceptible to impetigo and perihelia, commonly known as trench fever. There was a roaring trade in trench powder, which was not a standard army issue and had to be purchased by the Tommy. Vermijelli cost a shilling for a 1lb tin. It was mixed with water and smeared over the skin, but like many other professed vermin destroyers, it was quite ineffective and was another contemptible example of war profiteering.

Amidst all the deprivation, the darkness of trench humour flourished. Behind the lines, they constructed a makeshift concert hall. With a nod to Pediculus Vestmentii, it was called the Lice-um. (Pronounced "Lyceum" but there any similarity ended.) The Wipers Times was a newspaper produced in the trenches. An enterprising Captain Roberts had found a workable printing press in a delapidated building in the ruins of Ypres. Amazingly, they produced twenty-three irreverent issues from 1916 until the end of the war. One pseudo advert offering a cure for a dread disease typified the content:

ARE YOU SUFFERING FROM OPTIMISM?
Ask yourself the following questions:
DO YOU SUFFER FROM CHEERFULNESS?
Do you wake up thinking all is going well for the Allies?
Do you think our leaders are competent to win the war?

If the interrogated answered "Yes" to any of these questions, they were deemed to be in the clutches of the dread disease. It continued with a reassurance:
No need to worry though-
WE CAN CURE YOU
Two days spent at our establishment will effectively eradicate all traces of it from your system.

Cheerfulness was a rare commodity. For the beleaguered Tommy, death came in many forms. Like trench fever, trench foot was common and could carry a deadly payload. My children's maternal great grandfather, Frank Dexter, a Coldstream guard and three colleagues, were invalided out with trench foot in December 1916. They admitted the foursome to the Military Hospital in Halifax on Christmas Day where Frank would spend one hundred and twenty-three days recovering. None of his three colleagues survived.

Flies were a particular problem in summer, feasting on the unburied carcasses in No Man's Land. They could be spotted swarming like bees or a distant murmuration of starlings, ubiquitously landing on food and adding to the contamination.

Food in the trenches left a lot to be desired and little to be savoured. Maconochies Beef and Vegetable Stew was a euphemism for "fat and grizzle in a tin box" and was universally detested. Bully beef or pork and beans were a staple issue, often accompanied by army biscuits which were a bread baked until rock hard. So "durable" were these biscuits that a disgruntled private put a stamp on one and sent it home to his sweetheart, including a culinary "review" written on it. The biscuit actually arrived, and his wit was rewarded with eight days' detention! Ticklers Plum and Apple Jam were more popular and were known as "pozzy". By far, the most eagerly anticipated ration was the daily tot of rum, administered by the Sergeant Major using a spoon or the nose cone of an eighteen-pound shell, re-purposed to deliver the perfect dose. Rum was delivered to the front in earthenware jars stamped "SRD" which denoted Supply Reserve Depot, translated by wry humour to "Seldom Reaches Destination."

Napoleon had recognised that an army marches on its stomach but the tortured logistics of delivering food to the front meant that it was equally bad for the Germans. The commonality of the experience is clear in the similarity of the language. Low-quality butter, for example, was known as "axle grease" on one side of No Man's Land and "wagenschmiere" (wagongrease) on the other.

As we will examine in Chapter Six, British Army Command had determined that they take the war to the Germans. The demand for aggression included a directive to dominate No Man's Land. This had a profound effect on life in the trenches where nightfall would transform lethargic days into fevered activity. Under cover of darkness, the Tommies would seek to dominate No Man's Land through a mixture of activities which included wire cutting, trench raids, bombing parties and skirmishing. Night was very much a time of movement for the Germans as well. Patrolling. Repairing wire. Laying signal wires to intercept telephone messages.

The absence of shelling allowed the ears to attune to the steady cacophony of invisible noise sources. The double bass drone of heavy transport could be heard from behind their own and enemy lines as the instruments of death got replenished overnight. When there was no moonlight, both sides could get jittery and would frequently resort to the use of Verey lights. These were flares fired from a pistol which descended on a small parachute and would bathe the barren Somme landscape in bright green light for some seconds. The cumulative effect would have been epileptic and ethereal, rather like looking at disjointed, flickering pictures from a black and white film reel.

Against this backdrop, I can say with assurance that trench raids and bombing parties were two activities that carried exceptionally low life expectancy. I remember my grandfather telling me about his experience of a trench raid as we walked slowly back from Patterson's Corner.

They had sent me up to Crilly's Bar to fetch him home on a fine but frosty winter evening at around 8pm. My mother had previously been despatched for the purpose but had failed in her mission and my granny Lizzie (nee Forker) was getting more agitated, thus the introduction of the twelve-year-old grandson. I still vividly recall the scene as I opened the front door to the bar. Jimmy Crilly behind the bar in a tattered brown suit. Wispy auburn sidestrands under a balding pate and full bulbous lips, he cut a dark brooding figure as he languidly dried a glass. A roaring fire in the fireplace of the opposite wall, providing heat and most of the light in a flickering, gloomy room with the aroma of porter, whiskey, and pipe smoke. The rest of the scene was a clumsy reproduction. Two rows of chairs laid on their sides end to end with a one-yard gap between the rows. Five or six men sitting around the periphery supping their whiskey chasers (aka "bottles & halfuns") as they savoured the entertainment. Two men standing: the entertainers! One was Petsie Corr, the ringmaster and small-town smartass. Sadly, the other was my grandfather, coat off with a yard brush under his arm to mimic a rifle and about to re-enact an assault on a trench. Corr was just at the point of encouraging him to jump over the chairs (trench)

"How did you do it Andy? Show us again!"

Perhaps it was the wind from the door opening, or maybe he just wanted to see who the new customer was. Anyway, my grandfather looked round and our eyes locked. Nothing was said. They were taking the piss out of him. I saw it. He knew it. He may have been performing in the hopeful reward of a drink- probably was. "C'mon granda- lets go". He froze for a moment like a chess player pondering the position, then nodded and set the brush to one side. Despite Corr's exhortations for an encore, this show was over, and we walked out in silence. There was no need to finish his drink because he had no drink to finish. Petsie Corr is long since dead, but even after all these years, I still occasionally feel the urge to rip his ugly fucking head off.

As we trudged home slowly, my grandad in his long black coat and black felt hat, he recounted the story of being in a raid on German trenches at the Somme. Normally taciturn, maybe he wanted to disinfect the shame of the bar, or possibly it was just fresh in his mind, prodded by the floorshow. "I was showing them what we had to do when we raided German trenches" he explained. "I remember one time. Salty was the leader. Twenty-five of us. The order came through early in the afternoon. The Germans were digging a new trench in front of us. We were chosen to go out in the wee hours and kill anything in it. Salty handpicked his team. He picked me. He and two sergeants were on the periscopes all afternoon, working out a way through the wire."

Walking past Barney Corey's, he said "We didn't have much ground to cover- from about here to the house." Those who know Derryvale Road will appreciate that distance to be less than one hundred yards. Probably about seventy-five yards.

"Will ye tell them all tara!" boomed a disembodied voice from Barney's doorway, soon to be revealed as Barney himself when he stepped from the shadow.

"Is it yourself, Barney?"

"Has that big fella got you under arrest, Andy?" Barney Corey was a man perpetually in good humour.

Barney's fake concern brought a smile to my grandad's countenance, given he was a good foot taller than me.

"Aah now...Good night, Barney!"

A few paces further on we passed Cowboy Morgan's, and my grandad resumed his story.

"We got extra rations though nobody felt much like eating them. Salty and the two NCOs briefed us around 5.30pm. Two routes were identified in relation to a headless corpse hanging on the wire. German snipers had used his head for target practice until there was no head left." He had painted a gruesome picture. Some mother's son whose cadaver continued to serve King and country as a way marker, weeks after he should have had a decent burial.

"This raid was odd. Usually, I would carry some bombs in an apron, tied around me. This time I was only taking a rifle and bayonet. Everything had to be done quietly. No shouting as we left the trench. No noise. Over the parapet into their trench and bayonet as many as possible. Then back home. The whole job would take less than five minutes. When Salty stood up, that was our signal to follow him over the top. No whistle."

He murmured as if commentating while the events unfurled on a monitor. I remember feeling tension, not daring to interrupt him in case he stopped.

"At one point we stopped to let two wire cutters widen an opening. Eventually we got to the edge of their trench. We were about a dozen men abreast, in two rows. The lieutenant stood up and we all jumped up onto the parapet. The Germans had not completed the trench, and it was very shallow. They were mostly sat down, some lying asleep. I looked down into the shocked face of a German, blue eyes looking up at me. I rammed my bayonet down hard into his mouth, then tried to lift him as we had been taught in bayonet drill. Now there was lots of noise, shouting, screaming, shots. Salty was smashing the head of a German officer with his cudgel. There was not much space for fighting though we could use the butt of the rifle against the temple to finish some of them off. He ordered us back before their reinforcements came and we ran back as best we could. At the start, one of ours had lost his footing and went headfirst into the trench. He was dead with his feet above the parapet, like they were looking back at our trenches."

It was the only time he ever went into any detail. Whether the alcohol was allowing him to confront his horrors or drop his guard (with me), I do not know. But I don't think so; there was no shortage of alcohol. There was a drought of stories though.

"Twenty of us came back; we lost five. We reckoned up we killed thirty Germans. Salty was at high doh (in good spirits). Probably thinking it would get him his promotion to captain and more money. Willie Whiteley from the Moy slapped me on the back. Up Tyrone! It'll teach them to keep their dukes up!"

William Whitley was a private who, like Andy had enlisted at Armagh. He was killed on the 12th October 1916 in Burrows bodged operation. Frustratingly, I have found no trace of Lieutenant Salty. Derivatives like Salt, Saltay, Sault have all proven fruitless. My guess is that it was a nickname. One of our neighbours, Mickey Herron, in an ichthyic jibe was always known as "Salt Herron," certainly when he turned his back long enough. ("Herron" was the Tyrone pronunciation of "herring"- a fish popular in Lough Neagh.) There was a Lieutenant Pepper who, like Whitley, was killed in the 12th October debacle. Salty Pepper? The cutting edge of trench humour? We will never know.

Sassoon's poetic description of High Command as "incompetent swine" was a robust expostulation of a view that was widely held by the men in the trenches. No big surprise when one is routinely exposed to orders that take little cognisance of local conditions. In trench warfare, ineptitude had nowhere to hide. Often in Life, it is the small things that most grind. Inane Army rules being used by senior officers to reinforce their position in the command hierarchy will have been a frequent irritation.

One such King's Regulation demanded that the chin and the lower lip be shaved, but not the upper lip. Perhaps they thought it made it stiffer? A young Anthony Eden, a future Prime Minister, recounted the story of setting his platoon to repairing defences after a heavy all-night bombardment, only to be reprimanded by a senior officer for not having shaved by 9am as regulations demanded! Shaving the top lip was an even bigger crime which could bring the punishment of "cashiering" or ritual degradation on the parade ground. Sensibly, the Regulations changed during the war to prevent such an unfitting punishment.

In the front line, water invariably had to be transported in, so was usually in scant supply. Shaving in such circumstances was challenging, but it bequeathed a discipline that Andy Symington never lost. I can still picture in my mind's eye him hunching over a mirror outside the back door of Derryvale Road, stripped to the waist in winter or summer, shaving with a cut-throat razor and a small basin of water. His soaped-up wobbling brush laid to one side. Often accompanied by a rendition of "If you were the only girl in the world and I were the only boy". A two-song repertoire also included "I'll take you home again, Kathleen", another war time favourite.

Like my grandfather, the rank and file had no faith in their generals. Yet despite the widespread contempt for the tactics deployed, a sense of duty prevailed among the Tommies. Remarkably, when one considers the appalling conditions these human beings underwent, what emerged was a camaraderie based on a feeling of shared self-sacrifice and a bulldog spirit. Over a century later, that spirit continues to draw the most profound admiration. Putting it bluntly, the prevailing ethos was "our life is shit but no matter how bad it gets, together we will get through it because we are Brits". This indefatigable resilience is captured perfectly in a poem of the time: "The Spirit by Woodbine Willie". It was a simple ode using the most basic language, but with a characteristically patriotic sting in the tail:

"When there ain't no gal to kiss you, And the postman seems to miss you, And the fags have skipped an issue, Carry on.

When ye've got an empty belly, And the bulley's rotten smelly, And you are shivering like a jelly, Carry on.

When the Bosche has done your chum in, And the sergeant's done the rum in And there ain't no rations comin', Carry on.

When the world is red and reeking, And the shrapnel shells are shrieking, And your blood is slowly leaking, Carry on.

When the broken battered trenches, Are like the bloody butchers' benches, And the air is thick with stenches, Carry on.

Carry on, Though your pals are pale and wan, And the hope of life is gone, Carry on.

For to do more than you can, Is to be a British man, Not a rotten 'also ran', Carry on.

"Woodbine Willie" was the sobriquet given by the troops to Geoffrey Studdert-Kennedy, a remarkable character who merits a mention in our story. He was an army chaplain who routinely went unarmed into No Man's Land to dispense Woodbine cigarettes and spiritual support to wounded or dying soldiers. Born in Leeds to an Irish clergyman father, he was educated at Leeds Grammar School and Trinity College Dublin. Like many second-generation exiles (my son Ronan being a very fine example), he steadfastly maintained his Irishness throughout his life. A natural philanthropist, they estimated he gave away over 850,000 Woodbines funded through his army pay. The single-minded pursuit of his Ministry gave him a fearlessness which saw him awarded the Military Cross. As was customary, his citation appeared in the London Gazette:

"For conspicuous gallantry and devotion to duty. He showed the greatest courage and disregard for his own safety in attending to the wounded under heavy fire. He searched the shell holes for our own and enemy wounded, assisting them to the dressing station and his cheerfulness and endurance had a splendid effect upon all ranks in the front-line trenches, which he constantly visited."

As with my grandfather, the War took a heavy mental toll on Geoffrey Studdert-Kennedy and riling against the futility, he became a pacifist and an evangelist for the working classes. He was appalled by the post-war social inequality which "rewarded" men who had given selflessly in the trenches. In 1919 he wrote the tome "Lies", followed by "Food for the Fed Up" and "Democracy and the Dog Collar" (1921) which included a direct attack on the economic status quo- "Capitalism is Nothing but Greed, Grab and Profit-Mongering". He delivered his message through his work for the Industrial Christian Fellowship, swapping trenches for remote church halls as he pushed himself relentlessly, travelling all over Britain as an advocate for the working classes.

Sadly, his ministry ended prematurely with his death in Liverpool in 1929 aged forty-five. It says much for him that he emerged from the anonymising detritus of World War One to take his rightful place in the pantheon of the twentieth century "Clergy who made a Difference" with the likes of Martin Luther King, John Paul II, Mother Teresa and Father Denis Faul. He clearly lived his life fearlessly in the Word of God and embraced "Love thy neighbour" to extraordinary lengths. Although he had been vicar at St Edmund the Martyr in Lombard Street in the City of London, the Dean of Westminster who condemned him as a socialist refused him burial at Westminster Abbey, even though he never joined any political party.

In my first draft of this chapter, I remarked on the surprising lack of mutiny or rebellion given what these men had to endure and the manifest incompetence of their High Command. In reality, there were thought to be around fifty incidents of serious mutiny in the British Army during World War One. For tactical, morale, discipline and propaganda reasons, these were downplayed if not hushed up entirely at the time and that code of silence maintained long after the war had ended. One example of a story long suppressed concerned Lieutenant Colonel Arthur Loveband who was Commanding Officer of the Second Battalion Royal Dublin Fusiliers.

A career soldier, he joined the army in 1885 and saw action in the Boer War. He died on May 25th, 1915, during the Second Battle of Ypres on the third day of an engagement, which had seen the Battalion incur very heavy losses. On the morning of May 24th, the War Diary recorded the battalion strength at 17 officers and 651 other ranks. A heavy artillery bombardment the previous day had caused serious damage to the British defences, leaving a trench line that was indefensible. A chlorine gas attack on the evening of the 24th followed by sustained machine gunning of exposed troops had reduced the entire battalion to only two officers and 190 other ranks.

The War Diary notes "there was no surrender, no retirement and no quarter given or accepted." There are two ways of looking at this: the hoped for, official view that Loveband was a resolute, determined and courageous leader; or a darker reality that he was obdurate, brutal, reckless and stupid, sacrificing men in an indefensible position. That his battalion had lost 1,500 men in that month in total makes his leadership as indefensible as the line he was trying to hold. The War Diary records his death by a bullet to the heart as he spoke with officers outside his dugout. A contradictory report said he took a bullet through the top lip as he looked over the parapet. The truth was, he was beating his men with a blackthorn stick to encourage them to leave the trench in another hopeless counterattack when one of his own machine gunners had enough and shot him dead. Deliberately. With malice aforethought. And in so doing, he rid the world of a scoundrel.

The story of Loveband has long been suppressed. History's portrayal of him could not have been more juxtaposed with his behaviour in those last minutes. The official line, as the Kildare Observer obsequiously reported on the 5th of June following: "Seldom has the announcement of death, since the present terrible campaign first brought grief and mourning to an Irish family, been received with more general or genuine expressions of regret than that of Colonel Loveband, who fell valiantly in the midst of the regiment to which he was so endeared, in Flanders last week. No more popular officer, we venture to say, has ever led the gallant "Dublins" in the course of their long and brilliant record in the annals of British warfare, and no more popular commanding officer has ever been in charge of the depot in Naas."

To borrow from Voltaire, "History is no more than accepted fiction." He who holds the pen writes history.

For the final word on trench warfare, I will return to Siegfried Sassoon. A Jew who lies in an Anglican graveyard in Mells, Somerset near his Catholic clergyman mentor, Sassoon brilliantly captures the moment of these heroes "going over the top." His poem "Attack" is evocative and moving:

At Dawn the ridge emerges massed and dun In the wild purple of the glowering sun,

Smouldering through spouts of drifting smoke that shroud The menacing scarred slope; and one by one,

Tanks creep and topple forward to the wire The barrage roars and lifts. Then, clumsily bowed

With bombs and guns and shovels and battle gear, Men jostle and climb to meet the bristling fire.

Lines of grey, muttering faces, masked with fear, They leave their trenches, going over the top,

Whilst Time ticks blank and busy on their wrists, And Hope, with furtive eyes and grappling fists, Flounders in mud. O Jesus, make it stop!

5 LIONS LED BY ASSHOLES

The Institute of Directors (IOD) is an opulent Georgian sanctuary for the business community at the bottom of Pall Mall in London. Many gilded paintings adorn its imperious walls, including one of the British Military hierarchy during the First World War. Climb the deeply carpeted, dark oak staircase to the chandeliered first floor and there they stand in front of you. John Denton Pinkstone French ("Percy") wearing an ermine with Douglas Haig at his side, surrounded by a cohort of benighted, beknighted and generally double-barrelled worthies.

"General Officers of World War One" is the theme also preserved in oil by John Singer Sargent and hanging in the National Portrait Gallery. Capturing twenty-two of Military's finest in a fictitious congregation on the artist's easel, they stand in awkward caricature, an eternal monument to one of the most blundering leadership teams ever assembled. Spare a thought for those deemed too incompetent to be included like General Ian Hamilton whose mortifying efforts at Gallipoli demanded his exclusion. To parody the old soccer song: "how shit must he have been?" Still, he had Trenchard, Gough, Van Deventer and Munro for company, all of whom are conspicuous by their absence and confined to the same cupboard of embarrassment, whether through inability, incompetence or politics.

Looking at the twenty-two strong collective today and they are exactly what you see: a load of moustachioed old men in breeches and leather riding boots sporting an assortment of swords, anachronistic and hopelessly out of touch with their times. They forged their experience in an earlier century when the cavalry held sway. They reinforced it on the remote, open prairies of South Africa. Their inability to adapt their methods to the demands of trench warfare would cost almost one million lives, many of them lost needlessly. Adaptation and innovation would have been especially challenging for them, given their astonishing lack of diversity. These were a cadre of men drawn from a highly privileged sliver of society who shared the same upbringing, values, public schools and officer training corps, cemented in rigidity by the tired schooling of Sandhurst.

The appreciation of diversity, inclusion and continuous innovation was still a century away. These were men "who knew better", the products of a rigidly hierarchical society where army commissions were determined by birthright. Is it any wonder that such a group of "like-minded people" would agree on a policy of attrition to win the war? Their thinking was narrow, one-dimensional, antiquated and mutually reinforcing. It would have made little difference who was in charge. French's unparalleled losses at Ypres were soon trumped by Haig at the Somme, after all. Doing the same old things drew the same old results.

"The definition of insanity is doing the same thing over and over again and expecting a different result." – Albert Einstein

Haig took over from French in Dec 1915. Failure to press home a first day advantage at the Battle of Loos in September 1915 had caused a schism between French, Haig and Kitchener. Reinforcements, under the command of French did not arrive in time to support Haig's initial advance. French's subsequent decision to withdraw two of Kitchener's "New Army" divisions for further training showed where he intended the blame to sit. This opened the door to collusion between Haig and Kitchener, which left French isolated with nowhere to pass the unwanted baby. Exiled to Ireland as Lord Lieutenant, it freed French to peddle his incompetence in pursuit of another fine mess, which he would duly achieve some years later. Accompanied with promotion to viceroy, of course. The annals of British history would be hard pressed to find a more over-decorated under-achiever.

There have been some flimsy defences constructed for the army leadership. They tend to focus on how unprepared Britain was for war in 1914. They point at the comparatively small size of the army, which had barely eight divisions, the Navy being the chief defence of our island nations. No sizeable reserve army and a lack of investment in training left the generals with no choice but to "train on the job." While this line of argument could encourage sympathy for French in 1914-15, it provides no excuse for Haig in 1916.

The rout at Gallipoli had been a chastening experience and one of Haig's first decisions was to concentrate the war effort in France and Flanders. By ignoring Turkey, Austria-Hungary and Bulgaria, it gave him an influx of colonial troops from India, South Africa, Australia, New Zealand and Canada. This, combined with the impressive success of Kitchener's recruitment policy meant that Haig had numerical superiority on the Western Front with around one million men to deploy across thirty-eight infantry divisions in January 1916.

He determined to make the weight of numbers count. Attrition forced by aggression was the sum of his sterile thinking. After the early days of the Somme, Haig's diary reveals a change in his thinking. No longer any talk of a breakthrough, the measure of success shifted to the level of losses being inflicted on the Germans. Their losses must at least equate to our own. He recorded a deplorable attack on Delville Wood by the 49th Division, where their losses were less than a thousand! Haig's thinking reflected powerfully on his direct reports and persisted throughout the war. In September 1917, Rawlinson wrote in his diary how pleased Linford was that his division had lost 11,000 men in the previous two months. Casualties measured success.

"Winning by one wicket" was the dismal judgement of Haig's strategy widely held by the trench warriors and articulated by Willie Robins. Willie was one of two young South African brothers who would both tragically die at the Front within a year of each other, aged nineteen and twenty-one, respectively. Intelligent and thoughtful, Willie had to endure the loss of his younger brother Percy and the harrowing task of composing the letter home that would bring the awful news to his parents. You can sense the indescribable pain in his words when he explains that someone had removed Percy's wristwatch from the meagre collection of personal effects that were with him when he died. Apologising for not being able to return it, he tries to compensate his parents with the reassurance that his brother's most prized possession was his little bible and that thankfully was in the artefacts being returned to them.

Willie Robins was, like many of his antipodean colleagues, sceptical of the rigidly hierarchical British social and military culture. Raised as an independent thinker with a keen appreciation of God and humanity, his view from the trench was informed, direct and scathing:

"...this war will never end by fighting. Britain has got to find the man who can equal Hindenburg. Any man can do what Haig is doing now with the number of men and material at his disposal. The British high command badly wants reorganising. They are nothing but a lot of mugs with titles, money and whisky but no brains."

He expresses a sentiment which I believe was widely held among the "P.B.I." (poor bloody infantrymen):

"...the poor old British Tommy is taking his life in his hands and going through hell every day while those rotters sit twenty miles behind the line and sip their whisky and take all the credit and congratulations and CBs and KCMGs."

The latter two acronyms are knighthoods. "KCMG" for example stands for Knight Commander of St Michael & St George. It is extraordinary that such a young man like Robins could have such a clear set of views across society and military strategy, unhampered by the fog and mud of the trench. Like Tom Kettle, Willie Robins was a premature loss to humankind, the extent of which will never be known. He too would have made his mark, had he been allowed to live. Even from his lowly corporal perch, he could identify Germany's tactical superiority. For example, the lessons learned by the German defenders in the 1915 autumn battles were the value of "Defence in Depth". This is the term for a tactic whereby the defenders would man the Front Line lightly. This allowed the attacker initially to gain some ground beyond his own artillery cover in the opening phase of an attack. Only then to be counter-attacked by groups of well-placed defenders in second and third positions constructed behind the Front Line. This tactic persistently caused early offensive gains to be repelled by heavier losses.

In my opinion, based on my grandfather's input, it is safe to conclude that the average P.B.I. held his generals in contempt. As a humorous artefact to support this belief, we will once again turn to verse and a few stanzas penned by a young subaltern. The occasion was a trench inspection by the newly appointed commanding officer of the Royal Naval Division, General Sir Cameron Deane Shute KCB KCMG. Shute carried out a latrine inspection shortly after the Naval Division had "relieved" the Portuguese and found things to be in a particularly bad state of affairs. It is unclear whether this was because of the Portuguese or due to ablutionary practices at sea being less suited to the trench, but anyway, Shute was horrified and gave the men a stern dressing down.

Unfortunately for Shute, one of those subjected to his tirade was an Oxford graduate who would become a Member of Parliament and subsequently be recognised by PG Wodehouse as one of the best humourist writers of his era- A. P. Herbert. Herbert had a starred first in Jurisprudence from New College and possessed a prodigious intellect, backed by a scything sense of humour. As General Schute retreated to his chateau, Herbert reached for his pencil. The verses flowed:

> The General inspecting the trenches
> Exclaimed with a horrified shout
> 'I refuse to command a division
> Which leaves its excreta about.'
> But nobody took any notice
> No one was prepared to refute,
> That the presence of shit was congenial
> Compared to the presence of Shute.
> And certain responsible critics
> Made haste to reply to his words
> Observing that his staff advisors
> Consisted entirely of turds.
> For shit may be shot at odd corners
> And paper supplied there to suit,
> But a shit would be shot without mourners
> If somebody shot that shit Shute.

If wit was shit, A. P. Herbert would have had diarrhoea! His words became a popular song rendered with gusto throughout the army, much to the embarrassment of General Shute. Herbert became an independent MP for Oxford University from 1935 to 1950 when university constituencies were abolished. He wrote over fifty books and became renowned for using his wit to champion the underdog.

A jocular interjection but let us return to Haig and his strategy of attrition. In a war that had become static, physically and metaphorically sinking into the mud of Picardy and Flanders, a key part of his strategy was to dominate No Man's Land. Every officer commanding every inch of the front line was "encouraged" to take the fight to the enemy. "Am I as offensive as I can be?" was the mirror in which they encouraged officers to view their activities. Hunter-Weston had sacked officers whom he considered as being overly defensive, but he was a benign lightweight when compared to Brigadier General F.P. Crozier who had been known to execute summarily his own men in the trench. "There are times when local leaders can alter the situation by a display of firmness", he would euphemistically record in his memoirs.

Crozier was a controversial character. Almost devoid of normal human feelings, he was every inch a soldier and totally committed to winning based on unbreakable discipline. He ordered the execution of his own nephew who had fallen asleep on sentry duty. Knowing that most executions required the coup de grace from the officiating officer, he had dinner the night before with the subaltern assigned to the task. His nephew was successfully executed at dawn. As a Lieutenant Colonel, he led the 9th Battalion of the Royal Irish Rifles (36th Ulster Division) over the top on the fateful First of July 1916. In doing so, he directly ignored the orders of Haig and Co who had stipulated that ranks of Lieutenant Colonel and above were not to participate in the attack itself but were to retire to the safety of their dugouts. He was joined in this disobedience by the commander of the 10th Battalion, Lieutenant Colonel H C Bernard, and together they made a pact. If both were still alive, they would meet in No Man's Land and make any necessary alterations to the plan "which had come from high up in the hierarchy- and well back".

Crozier took an additional initiative which contravened regulations. He led his men out of the trenches two minutes before the end of the barrage. This allowed his men to reduce the amount of No Man's Land they had to cover and so engage sooner with the enemy.

Within a few minutes of going over the top, Crozier saw Bernard getting killed and fulfilled his commitment in the pact by assuming command of Bernard's 10th battalion besides his own. With a first-hand view, Crozier directed the advance in real time, identifying holes in the wire and advancing multiple small groups through them while the barrage was continuing, thus giving the Germans much less time to react. Like him or loathe him, he deserves considerable credit for his role in the outstanding performance of the 36th Division on that day. By flying in the face of High Command's policy of trying to lead from (a long way in) the rear, he had brutally exposed the shortcomings of their distanced leadership. He had shown that the plans of "the fighting front" were far more effective.

And here is the crux of it: he exposed the absurdity of an army commander being able to dictate to a battalion commander his conduct during the heat of battle. Time after time after time, they issued orders from Haig's base in Montreuil which took no cognisance of local conditions. It also exposed a serious tactical weakness. There was inadequate co-operation between infantry and artillery. Later in the war, infantry could communicate with the artillery command to modify their barrage, for example, to pinpoint a troublesome machine gun nest.

In the aftermath of World War One, the government and the King went to considerable efforts to represent Haig and the war effort positively. Conan Doyle and Buchan produced very loyal tomes to disguise the bloodshed as a patriotic sacrifice that was necessary and not wasted. Apologists for Haig and his cohorts point to the inexperience of the British army, constraints imposed by the coalition with France, general lack of preparedness for war and rapid progress in developing new weaponry. While these carry an amount of validity, the views of the apologists should be dismissed. The human and economic disaster of World War One rests squarely and solely with the military leadership and their sustained ineptitude, ignorance and obstinacy.

Britain's greatest wartime leader, Churchill, was unequivocal in his criticism of the Somme offensive, where he saw the enormous loss of life for gains measured in yards as simply not worth the effort. He lobbied the entire war cabinet (of which he was not a member), questioning the validity of continuing with a strategy which would waste so many lives in vain. Although ignored at the time (and decried by George V as a troublemaker), Churchill's wisdom was rewarded in 1919 with his appointment to the cabinet as Secretary for War.

Even the aforementioned Brigadier General F.P. Crozier, in his book "Men I have Killed" is scathing in his condemnation of High Command. He describes Rawlinson as a circus clown; Robertson, as a good troop sergeant major and asserts that both Haig and French would have been shot by their own troops given the opportunity. He also underlines the fact that the German army remained unbeaten, and the war only ended because the German population was starving to death. Thus, he reinforces Churchill's assertion that Britain should have prosecuted the war differently. Different tactics could have won with much less bloodshed.

We began this chapter in Pall Mall at the Institute of Directors and there we will return. The ground floor Directors Room at the IOD contains a compendium of individual portraits of esteemed British warriors including Haig, his henchman Robertson, Kitchener and Jellicoe from our period of interest. Down here, there is even space for Trenchard. There is a somewhat surprising inclusion, however. Standing arms folded and staring defiantly across the lavishly appointed room is none other than His Imperial Majesty Wilhelm II of Germany. Kaiser Bill! The ninth King of Prussia and third Emperor of Germany who had been Commander-in-Chief of the German forces throughout the First World War! Kaiser Bill's granny was, of course Queen Victoria and King George V his first cousin. Looking back through history, it surprised me how esteemed the German Royal Family were in the UK. In 1902, at the height of the Boer War, one provincial newspaper railed against the "pestilential mendacities" being levelled by some German diplomats at the British Army treatment of Boer women and children. (History now accepts the atrocities committed in British concentration camps). The article proceeded:

"If so logical a people as the Germans will believe the ill-garnished stories, despite the fact that their Emperor holds the highest rank in the army so dishonoured…We owe an apology to the German Emperor for introducing his august name in connection with this nauseous topic. <u>But the Emperor is one of us.</u> He is an Admiral of the British Fleet, a Field Marshal of the British Army".

Having established his military credentials, the article pays homage to his outstanding character:

"He is more than that. He is a soldier from whose untarnished reputation, honour is brilliantly reflected. He is a chivalrous, generous hearted gentleman".

And of course, it offers the only sane conclusion:

"If he believed that his comrades of the British Army had stained their flag with the horrors that have been charged on them, is it likely that he would continue to wear the uniform of that disgraced army?"

Over two million souls sacrificed in a family tiff. An intra-family point of honour. This is too simplistic a judgement, but the persistent thought remains that surely the respective Royals could have collaborated to prevent further loss, once the scales of bloodshed and impasse became clear?

In 1787, Thomas Jefferson had expressed the opinion:

"The tree of Liberty must be refreshed from time to time with the blood of patriots and tyrants."

He presciently did not include Royals. Kaiser Bill's son, Prince Wilhelm, was a field commander on the Western Front from 1914 and survived the experience. The cost of defeat was enforced abdication and exile in Holland. No blue blood was spilled in the ocean of red.

In assessing British army military strategy in World War One, the only conclusion that can be drawn is that the generals who presided over this unparalleled human disaster were completely incompetent. Ineptitude on an unprecedented scale. It is perhaps fitting to leave the last word on their tactics with those who had witnessed them most closely. From a few hundred yards across No

Man's Land, the views of the Germans are enlightening. Stefan Westmann, the German Medical Officer involved in that heartening handover of the wounded on July 5th, recorded the following in his diary on the evening of July 1st (the first day of the Battle of the Somme which had seen fifty thousand British casualties including nineteen thousand fatalities):

"The British generals had not yet learned that it was useless to let human beings run against machine guns and intense artillery fire, even after softening up."

Contrast this view with Haig's that the same nineteen thousand, Day One losses "cannot be considered severe." Another astonished German officer could not believe his eyes in the first moments of an attack as he saw the heavily laden Tommies walking slowly towards him.

"It looked like they were on a day's outing! Some were even carrying picnic baskets and others Kodaks as if to take photographs as a souvenir of their outing."

The "picnic baskets" contained pigeons and the "Kodaks" were power buzzers. These were but two elements in the arsenal of communication devices and assorted paraphernalia, which the under fire P.B.I. had to shoulder to compensate for the communication gap with generals twenty miles away from the action. How on Earth were they ever going to cart that extra baggage through barbed wire, over mud and across shell holes...and survive? In the final minutes before the whistle to go over the top, these men knew they were facing almost certain death. How long now, sir? Three minutes. How long now, sir? Two minutes. Final puffs on fags. One last exhortation to God for a safe deliverance as hope fought fear. A shrill peep unleashing an instantaneous convulsion of courage...

While acknowledging the bravery of the common Tommy, the contempt of German General Erich Luddendorf for Haig and his senior leadership team is palpable:

"The English Generals are wanting in strategy. We should have no chance if they possessed as much science as their officers and men had of courage and bravery. They are lions led by donkeys."

The "lions led by donkeys" analogy is one first coined during the Crimean War. "L'armée anglaise est une armée de lions, commandée par des ânes." Literally translated "the English army is an army of lions, commanded by asses."

In my mind's eye, I gaze once more at John Singer Sargent's portrait and conclude the literal translation to be more appropriate, on the whole...

6. FIT FOR HEROES

David Lloyd George, the sitting Prime Minister, made a speech in Wolverhampton on November 23, 1918. In it, he said the task facing them was "to make Britain a fit country for heroes to live in." In the economic and social shambles that prevailed post-Armistice, no ambition could have been loftier or indeed, more doomed to fail. The cynic will say that he had one eye on his forthcoming re-election. Or that his words were the worried response to the possibility of a Russian copycat revolution when several million demobilised soldiers transferred to the ranks of the unemployed. Men who had given everything, returning to nothing. Looking at his role in delivering the Insurance Act of 1908, Lloyd George was certainly a libertarian and a man with a social conscience. So I, for one, would be inclined to accept the bona fides of his intentions. Whether he ever could deliver, and indeed the degree to which he could deliver, are legitimate questions. Economics really was the science of scarcity, and it dealt him a poor hand. The cost of the War had bankrupted the country.

The disastrous economic state of Britain was not immediately apparent directly after the war, as the economy enjoyed a short-term boom. This enabled the Welsh Wizard to marshall the Tories behind the Unemployment Insurance Act, which passed in 1920, effectively creating the "dole." Unemployed workers received a payout for fifteen weeks (fifteen shillings for a man, twelve shillings for a woman.) There were some restrictions, but it still applied to a wide cadre of eleven million workers. Unfortunately, unemployment reached record levels the following year and the cost to the Treasury soared, putting Lloyd George in an invidious position and forcing him to compromise on his libertarian ideals.

Britain's pursuit of victory at any cost had transformed the country from a world power with investments, industrial leadership and influence across the globe into an indebted nation. An indebted nation that had sacrificed the flower of its manhood. Lengthy memorial plaques in every college in Oxford and Cambridge bear testament to the talent squandered. Now, when the country really needed picking up by its bootstraps, the talent simply was not there.

Whole industries disappeared never to return. For example, in 1914, Camden in London was the epicentre of global piano production - such was the destruction of the infrastructures, expertise and skills that it just never returned. Military imperatives had dictated that Britain's entire production capability diverted to support the war effort. Forced to look elsewhere, Britain's customers went to competing nations who had more efficient infrastructure and modern techniques. After the war, many of these clients did not return, with devastating effects on demand for iron, steel, coal, textiles and shipbuilding. The result was economic stagnation with 1921 seeing deflation and the decade of the Roaring Twenties typically experiencing unemployment levels around 10%.

From this bleak terrain, Lloyd George was trying to craft a land fit for heroes. He would focus on three key areas: housing, pensions and employment.

Housing

Pre-war housing in cities and towns consisted mainly of rows of small houses located back-to-back in a highly congested configuration. Built close to factories to satisfy the need for cheap labour generated by the Industrial Revolution, houses were cheap, cramped, and lacked basic amenities. They were essentially slums. Mill Row in Brackaville was a typical example. Built to house labour for the adjacent Roan Spinning Mill, it was condemned as unfit for human habitation and demolished in the early 1960s. Today all that remains is a small field forming part of a mini golf course: one can't imagine that it once held thirty houses and upwards of 250 people.

The upper echelons of British Society, the Landed Gentry with most to lose in the event of "social turmoil", were unnerved by the Russian Revolution. They worried about what might happen if the returning heroes were forced back into the slums they had swapped for the Somme. Equally, a powerful undercurrent of discontent prevailed among those who had fought at the front. Giles Eyre captures these feelings in his outstanding book "Somme Harvest- Memories of a P.B.I. in the Summer of 1916." The P.B.I acronym stands for "Poor Bloody Infantryman" and Eyre eloquently describes the pervading dissatisfaction of the frontline soldier with those who had stayed behind and profiteered from their misery and sacrifice.

The whiff of a fast buck still brought out the worst in human nature and there were many episodes of skulduggery inconsistent with a country united in a war effort. Inconsistent and shameful. One such example came to be known as the Glasgow Rent Strike.

With most able-bodied men thrust into khaki and serving at the front while their families remained at home, there was an influx of labour into the city to fill the newly vacant jobs in the shipyards and factories now producing essentials to support the war. The newcomers needed somewhere to live, and this created extra demand

and the opportunity to raise rents. In an era of very low owner occupancy and when council houses had not yet been invented, rental properties were entirely in the private sector and the result was an across-the-board increase in rents of twenty-five per cent. Thus, the wives of men at the front risking their lives, with no increase in income, were being coerced into higher rentals to remain in their slums. The landlords thought these isolated women were a soft touch. They embarked on a process of harassment and threatened evictions. Had they asked me, I would have told them that Glasgow women are made of sterner stuff. So it proved.

Enter the fray one Mary Barbour. A housewife from Govan, Mary saw their twenty-five per cent uplift demand and made a counteroffer-

"We will give you nothing!"

The "Glasgow Rent Strike" was conceived in Mary's scullery. She galvanised the resistance and took the fight to the bailiffs. Whenever a bailiff was spied in the tenement, an alarm sounded and every woman would drop what she was doing, rush to the point of alarm and pelt the bailiff with whatever missile came to hand. Bags of flour were a particular favourite. There were humiliating incidents of tough bailiffs having their trousers removed before being evicted back onto the street, left to take the walk of shame back to the office for an uncomfortable "debrief" with the boss...

"Did ye get the rent?"

Under Mary's direction, the resistance strengthened, reaching its zenith in November 1915 when she led twenty thousand in a peaceful protest to a magistrate's court where some rent defaulters were being prosecuted. Not only was her movement growing, but it also was spreading to other cities. "Mrs Barbour's Army" was too powerful for the authorities and Lloyd George stepped in as smartly as a referee would stop a fight to prevent further punishment. Within a month, the Rents & Mortgages Restriction Act was passed, which fixed rents for the duration of the war at pre-1914 levels. Mary Barbour was elected to Glasgow Council as a Labour Councillor in 1920 and became one of the first women to serve as a magistrate in 1927. She became a force for women's rights after the war and established the first Family Planning centre in Glasgow. Over a century later, they erected a statue to her in Govan in a fitting memorial to an indomitable spirit.

With rents fixed at a level that would not attract private capital, Lloyd George pondered the problem of how to fund good quality, affordable houses for the returning heroes. He hit upon an ingenious solution which was passed into legislation in July 1919 as the Housing and Town Planning Act. By empowering local authorities to build houses and providing governmental cover for any losses, he was eliminating the profits taken by landlords and mortgage providers and thus enabling better quality housing at lower rents. The "council house" was born!

The Act tasked every local authority with creating a plan to provide housing for the working classes. The Tudor Walters Report, released in late 1918, provided guidance on what forms the housing could take to achieve the basic principles of proper sanitation, light, individual bedrooms and garden space. A very influential report which would define house building for over forty years, the Tudor Walters provided blueprints for three different "Ex-Servicemen's Cottages". The most compact had a floor-space of 850 square feet with a living room, separate scullery and two bedrooms upstairs. The next size provided a separate bathroom, while the largest provided 1,050 square feet and featured an upstairs bathroom and three bedrooms. Such was the loftiness of 1919 ambition that these sizes were stipulated as the minimum, although economic pressures changed these to maxima by 1922.

Another key guideline was on the density of new housing estates with a maximum of twelve houses per acre in cities and eight per acre in the country. By contrast, Victorian slums had between forty and eighty houses per acre. The Addison Act was duly passed in 1919 to implement the Tudor Owen recommendations. In Ireland, The Irish Land (Provision for Sailors and Soldiers) Act became law in the same timescale and with the same aim.

The Irish initiative was somewhat complicated by a guerrilla war, independence, civil war and partition (a nod of acknowledgement for my grandfather's contribution to the complexity) but astonishingly the Irish Sailors and Soldiers Land Trust (ILLST) took all this in its stride! A tripartite body with members appointed by the London, Dublin and Belfast governments, the ILLST would build over four thousand cottages for ex-servicemen in the 1920s and 1930s. In Tyrone, they built one hundred and twenty-seven cottages at thirty-two locations, the first of which was completed at Glebe townland outside Cookstown in October 1921. Derryvale Road in Brackaville was one of the thirty-two locations and a three-acre plot of land was purchased from the local mill (Roan Spinning Mill) for the princely sum of two hundred and twenty-five pounds and nine shillings. At today's valuations, this approximated to £13,000 and "looked a good buy" as locals like Hugh Pat McNally or Tommy Braden may well have opined at the adjacent Patterson's Public House, over a Black Bush and bottle of stout.

This was a greenfield development from the top of Mill Row Hill to the crossroads at Pattersons Corner, on the opposite side of the road. Five houses were built on the comparatively spacious plot: four of ILLST type two and one type six. Type two denoted semidetached and type six was a detached house set in just over half an acre, which I am proud to say became my grandfather's house and remains in the family to this day. Construction completed on October 24th, 1924, and the rent was set at four shillings and sixpence. Galbraith and Toner occupied the semis next door to my grandad's and the second pair, at the corner opposite the pub, went to Bradley and McIlvenna. Five heroes had been housed.

Some forty years later, the ILLST would offer these cottages for sale to the occupiers at substantially reduced rates. By the mid-1960s, rents had steadily increased to thirteen shillings and seven pence (13s 7d) and some houses were offered at £570 against an estimated market value of £1,800. Of course, many were snapped up, including 32 Derryvale Road, as my grandfather grasped the opportunity of owner occupancy and joined the landed classes. His father, Matthew, who had died in 1933, would have marvelled at this turn of events from his celestial perch. For Matthew, house and land ownership were unattainable and would have exceeded the boundaries of imagination.

Pensions

Andy Symington was discharged due to wounds on 21 August 1917 with the award of the Silver War Badge number 226570. He was adjudged to have 50 per cent disability, which meant that he received a pension of 32 shillings (£1.60 in modern money). The level of disability was continuously reviewed, and his pension entitlement reduced to twenty shillings (£1) in April 1920. There was still a taboo about mental illness, despite 80,000 men being diagnosed with shellshock by the end of the war.

In 1920, a Parliamentary 'root and branch' investigation of the causes and treatment of 'shellshock was set up and reported in June 1922. The all-male, conservative, middle and upper class, committee interviewed only six servicemen, although over 60,000 were drawing disability pensions for mental ill-health and 9,000 were still under treatment. It concluded that the term 'shellshock' should no longer be applied as a diagnosis and soldiers suffering with concussion should be defined as battle casualties whilst those with neuroses should not. The significance being that the latter would therefore be ineligible for a pension, thus reducing the states' liabilities. The report quoted an unattributed "well known" doctor as saying that many recruits were already neurotics and did not want to serve, effectively branding them cowards.

Although returning shellshocked soldiers constituted a specific subgroup, their situation also illustrates the wider difficulties of Great War returnees. Whether disabled or fully fit, each veteran faced an Olympic hurdle race related to their psychological and social readjustment to civilian society. War neurotic ex-servicemen faced two areas of difficulty. Like all returnees, they faced a large and unwieldy bureaucracy that paid little attention to the needs of individuals. Second, Ministry of Pensions policy for war neurotic ex-servicemen, guided by Sir John Collie, exacerbated the faults in the system.

Substantial political objectives were implicit in the establishment of the Ministry of Pensions, not least the appointment of Collie – an influential expert on malingering – as one of its leading authorities. The titles of some of Collie's previous publications are revealing. Detecting fraud in insurance claims; "Malingering" and "the Psychology of the Fraudulent Mind" leaves little doubt where his mind stood. His approach conveniently fitted into the government's agenda. Its objectives were to uphold and support a restrictive military view of shellshock and thereby limit financial liability; and, above all, to preserve the existing distribution of wealth while retaining a posture of public concern.

Collie may have been a well-educated, socially privileged authority on fraudulent minds, but he needed to get out of bed earlier to keep up with my grandfather. There are six pension records attributed to Andy Symington (he had clearly inherited his father's enthusiasm for pensions)! They were initially paid to an address in Glenboig in Lanarkshire, then Red Row in Kettle Lane, Brackaville and finally c/o L Quinn, Motor Agent in Athlone. The Athlone address would have been a tactical compulsion given he was wanted by the authorities (Black & Tans and B-Men) in Tyrone and of course, his service base in Collins army was in Athlone (Custume Barracks). This is consistent with a man "on the run" but he also managed to claim a Grant by Military Service (Civil Liabilities) which gained him £50 in August 1920. The purpose of the grant was to fund a horse and cart to start a career as a hawker, a job he would do for over thirty years. He sold fish around Brackaville, Newmills, Stewartstown, and Coalisland, which he sourced at Maghery on the shores of Lough Neagh. Interestingly, this grant was paid to his Brackaville address, which confirms that his "most wanted" status came after August 1920, early 1922 in fact.

There were no flies on Andy Symington!

Employment

Lloyd George was acutely aware of the structural unemployment that would emerge from Britain's decrepit heavy industries. He tried to introduce measures in mitigation. The Trade Facilities Act 1921 created government-backed loans to industry, designed to encourage investment and stave off bankruptcy. Subsidies and grants were provided to mining and shipbuilding to absorb surplus labour. Tariffs were introduced as he sought to protect indigenous companies from international competition. He also started the Overseas Trade Department to promote and financially assist exports.

He passed several measures designed to ease labour disputes and reduce strikes. The Industrial Courts Act of 1919 being a good example.

Despite his best intentions, the promises in his fine rhetoric of 1918 foundered on the curmudgeonly reality of 1921. On top of it all, as covered elsewhere, the highest level of unemployment that had ever been seen in the UK. Spiralling costs and a bankrupt economy left him no room for any fancy footwork. In August 1921, he reluctantly appointed Sir Eric Geddes to identify savings within government. "The Geddes Axe" would soon enter folklore. Its wielding would cut Lloyd George down to size.

In my opinion, despite his bullying treatment of Michael Collins, Lloyd George is one of the greatest British prime ministers. He laid the foundations of the Welfare State and sought to achieve a fairer society. He awarded farmland and urban allotments to returning veterans. He granted women the right to become lawyers, accountants and vets, professions from which they had been excluded. With foresight, he created the Forestry Commission, the first public body dedicated to protecting our countryside. Council houses, pensions and unemployment benefits are the standout achievements in his undoubted commitment to the working class.

It is ironic that he is the only Prime Minister ever who spoke English as a second language.

7 THE MIRACLE OF LIFE

Around six million men served in the British Army during the First World War. Over 800,000 lost their lives. The wounded, blinded, crippled and insane numbered over two million. Geoffrey Caiger-Watson, my daughter-in-law's grandfather, was a twenty-year-old second lieutenant when he transferred to the First Battalion of the Royal Irish Fusiliers on 25th October 1916. Andy Symington, my grandfather, was a twenty-four-year-old private who had survived four months on the Somme and had effectively seen it through to its stalemate conclusion. That they served in the same battalion defies probability.

More than that, they fought together for two months until Geoffrey returned to England at the end of that year on sick leave. During these closing weeks of 1916, the First Battalion headcount was so depleted, they must have known each other. From then, the fates of these two warriors overlapped and intertwined. Geoffrey returned to the First Battalion on May 17th, 1917, too late to re-unite him with Andy who was on the Casualty List at the end of March, prior to his discharge in August. It is unlikely they ever met after that. Yet, over a century later, their lineages would converge in a miracle called Findlay.

Andy's great grandson, Ronan James Ferguson, had married Geoffrey's granddaughter, Stephanie, on Friday 13th July 2018, the Cupidian destination of a chance meeting on a train. Their first born, Findlay, was not a man to be rushed and duly entered the world on March 7th, 2022. In some celestial Elysium, a dashing lieutenant and a seasoned fighter would have been high fiveing! Wait, no…I see it clearer now…they are charging their glasses! They are toasting the Miracle of Life, uniquely dependent on them BOTH surviving the trenches. Had either of them succumbed, Findlay would not be. No matter how challenged your beliefs, sometimes in life one can sense the Hand of God.

For now, let us turn our attention to Findlay's maternal great grandfather. Geoffrey Caiger-Watson was a remarkable man. Absolutely remarkable. He was born in Brighton on May 13, 1896. After studying art and figure drawing at the Brighton School of Arts in 1912-13, he joined the Inland Revenue as a clerk. At the outbreak of war, he enrolled in the Sussex Yeomanry (a territorial unit) but was quickly identified and sent to the Inns of Court OTC (Officer Training Corps) for officer training. Hardly surprising, as Geoffrey had come from a family with a military tradition. His older brother, Aubrey, was a lieutenant (and eventually captain) in Russell's Infantry, an Indian regiment where he spent six years before demobilisation in 1920. In fact, Aubrey was also assigned to the Faughs for a period in 1917. His grandfather, James Caiger-Watson, was born in 1828 in Athlone. As Athlone was a garrison town for the British army since its construction in 1691, it is highly likely that his father (Geoffrey's great grandfather) was stationed there in the same Custume Barracks where almost one hundred years later, Lieutenant Andy Symington would march into in 1922 on the creation of the Irish Free State.

Geoffrey's officer training saw him spend two months in Berkhamsted in Hertfordshire with other potential officers where they would dig trenches on the Common (some of which are still visible to this day.) Geoffrey was one of the first of almost 12,000 recruits to pass through the Berkhamsted process: by 1918, over 2,000 were dead and almost half suffered serious wounds. Confirmed as a second lieutenant in late September 1915, which earned him a posting to France in early July 1916, he transferred to my grandfather's First Battalion in late October. He joined a threadbare battalion, which had incurred brutal losses earlier that month.

On the 12th, High Command ordered them over the top in a typically ill-considered assault on enemy strongholds between Le Transloy and Les

Boeufs. Lacking any coherent planning, the operation was a monument to incompetence and cover up. Brigadier General A R Burrowes, who gave the order to attack, noted in his diary that there had been "considerable work in removing the wounded left from previous fighting". He confirmed the arrangements were finally in place at 4am on the morning of the attack. No consideration was given to whether the men were ready for battle. The Regimental Diary also reveals that the attack order was only issued at 9.30pm. After a fine dinner, a decent claret and a few whiskies, perchance? One can only conclude, in the light of what followed, that this was a rushed and reckless operation.

At 2.05pm, the Faughs left the trenches simultaneously as the artillery launched a creeping barrage, both following the plan of High Command. The undisputed fact is that the infantrymen were decimated by their own shells. Added to that, the machine guns in the German front lines, which were supposed to have been taken out by an earlier bombardment, remained unscathed and ruthlessly operational.

The results were devastating. One week earlier, battalion strength was recorded at 24 officers and 825 other ranks. On October 13th, only 5 officers and 209 other ranks remained. Of the four companies, "A" company had no officers and only

39 other ranks. That was all that was left. Yet Andy Symington still stood! Somehow, he had survived. This was the beleaguered crew that Geoffrey joined as they billeted in Corbie in the pouring rain of a miserable late October day. The mood will have been indescribably heavy, like the bedraggled in a waiting room for Hell.

The cover up in the Battalion's diary defies belief. The official line once again blamed the men! At 2.5pm, they had left the trenches "in great style". "Such was their enthusiasm to engage that they caught up with the creeping barrage, which inflicted losses." Quite unbelievable!! "This forced them to pause, and, in that delay, the Germans returned to their trenches with their machine guns." Three hundred and eighty-five dead, but no fault of the generals.

Fortunately for Geoffrey and Andy, November was a quiet month, spent mainly in training. It teemed with rain and turned cold towards the end of the month, a harbinger of the hard winter that followed. The Battle of the Somme was over. News coverage had moved on to the death of Emperor Franz Joseph of Austria-Hungary. Many diarists acknowledged December was the worst month spent in the trenches. Trench foot was of epidemic proportions. In appalling weather, a new trench line was being cut through ground that had already hosted earlier fighting. Swollen, rheumatic hands were forced to dig trenches through the burial grounds of previously fallen comrades. The Devil himself could not have invented a more heinous torture for this collection of unfortunates. Yet here, in 900 yards of the vilest trenches near Fregicourt, south of Saillisel and east of the Bapaume-Peronne road - here, as they stood thigh deep in freezing water, here amidst the muck and detritus we find the glistening diamond of our tale...

We have referred elsewhere to the story of Andy lying injured in No-Mans-Land and owing his life to the order of a wounded officer that his stretcher bearers also pick up Symington—"he's a good 'un." There is material to suggest that the officer was none other than Second Lieutenant Geoffrey Caiger- Watson!

Consider the evidence:

1. Both were in that wretched half mile of trench in December, 1916.

2. Geoffrey suffered gunshot wounds around Dec 12th, which resulted in him being invalided to England for almost three months- confirmed by hospital records.

3. Battalion records show a total presence of six officers and 243 other ranks.

4. Geoffrey was one of six officers, but the fact that he was wounded (not killed or unharmed) reduces the subset further ...to a subset of one??

While it may not pass the legal test of reasonable doubt, I find it incredulous that what started out as a relationship between two men in an army of 6 million, has boiled down to two men in one handful. I again sense the Hand of God and return my thoughts to the miracle that is Findlay.

Geoffrey returned to the Faughs on May 17, 1917, remaining with the battalion until the 9th of June 1918 when he took a post in the nascent Royal Air Force. Before he left, however, he won the Military Cross for gallantry in February 1918. Employed as an intelligence officer, his job was to report to High Command on the state and deployment of our troops. In the chaos of battle with communication lines destroyed, the only way to understand what was going on was to visit the remote trenches and look for yourself! This "intelligence gathering" was a highly precarious occupation. One could easily be shot by your own side or leap into a trench that had fallen to the Germans. As customary, the London Gazette published his citation for the Military Cross. It read: "2nd Lieut Geoffrey Caiger-Watson, R.Ir.Fus For conspicuous gallantry and devotion to duty as an intelligence officer during operations. He carried out his duties with great success under the most difficult conditions. On one occasion, he went over the top under heavy machine gun fire to get into touch with isolated positions. His accurate reports and untiring energy were of the greatest value to the battalion."

On joining the Royal Air Force, Geoffrey undertook a series of training courses over a three-month period. He studied Aeronautics at Reading; Aerial Gunnery at Hythe and New Romney before graduating from Wireless and Observation school in Uxbridge and Winchester. Qualified as a RAF Observer (for the uninitiated, the observer is the guy in the back seat behind the pilot), his new role returned him to France in late September 1918, in the dying embers of the war. Seeing things out quietly was never in his script and at the very end of the war, he was involved in an incident caused by an error of judgement borne of inexperience. The incident almost cost him his life and killed his 18-year-old pilot.

I am indebted to Monsieur Jacques de Ceuninck, a Belgian national, for providing me with the details and materials on the case we are about to relate. Mr de Ceuninck's father-in-law was a seven-year-old boy who had a ringside seat as the action unfolded. It was about 10.30am on November 9th, 1918. World War One would end within two days.

Geoffrey was flying in an RE8, a single-engine, two-seater plane with a top speed of 150 kmh. Developed for the Royal Flying Corps in 1916, this represented groundbreaking technology and offered considerable versatility: if the rear machine gun was removed, two 50kg bombs could be loaded in its place! His pilot was John George Leckenby, by all accounts a highly talented 18-year-old who had just come through aeronautic school "with flying colours". Born in Hull but resident in Norwich, he was tipped to have a very bright future.

The duties of an observer doubled up to include rear machine gunner and so it was that our crew decided to engage with a party of six German hussars on horseback, near the village of Escanaffles, northeast of Celles. Leckenby flew low over the farm of the Depoorter family to begin the engagement, allowing Geoffrey to fire a noisy opening salvo, etched forever in the memory of the seven-year-old witness. As they wheeled to re-engage, a wing clipped a tree, causing the plane to crash and burst into flames in a field across the road from the farmhouse. John Leckenby was killed instantly. A bright future snuffed like a candle. Geoffrey suffered a fractured skull, broken leg and was badly burned. He owed his life to a local couple, Michel and Lequenne Tonneau who bravely pulled him from the burning wreckage, despite the flames and the roar of exploding machine gun cartridges. Fortunately, the Hussars continued on their way without a backward glance. Sadly, they would all die the following day in another machine gun attack. The RE8 was completely destroyed in the inferno.

There were no hospitals, doctors, or medicine, so the Depoorter family could only take Geoffrey in and make him as comfortable as possible. Marie Depoorter, the 16-year-old daughter, gave a statement in which she recalled how handsome the injured airman was, with shining dark hair and white teeth. They found his wallet amid the strewn debris, which showed that he was due to be married. (In fact, Geoffrey had married Phyllis Rebecca Peters earlier that year while recuperating in Brighton). The Depoorter family gave Leckenby as decent a burial as they could, using a plank and draping the body in a tarpaulin. The family then cared for Geoffrey for two days until the British army came and picked him up, taking him back to their field hospital for much needed medication and treatment. John Leckenby's body was exhumed the following year and re-buried in a Commonwealth War Grave in the cemetery at Escanaffles. By the thinnest of margins, Leckenby died, and Caiger-Watson lived, thanks to the bravery of the Tonneaux.

Geoffrey was repatriated to England on December 7th, where he spent eighteen months recovering from his injuries. His spirit was indomitable and after a brief period in the Records Office at York (long enough to learn that such work was not for him), this adrenaline junkie joined the West African Frontier Force and so began a lifelong love affair with Africa. That period of his life is outside our scope, though worthy of a book and indeed a film on its own merits. Highlights include becoming fluent in Hausa (one of the major Nigerian languages) and several other African languages; marrying a Nigerian princess and receiving the OBE for services to Anglo-Nigerian relations in the New Years Honours List of 1978. At the outbreak of World War 2, aged forty-three, he signed up again and was posted as adjutant to the infantry training centre of the Royal Irish Fusiliers. The training role was too sedentary for his metabolism and before the end of 1940, he had returned to Africa where he served as a captain in the Nigeria regiment. By any standards, in any era of history, Geoffrey Caiger-Watson was a remarkable human being, a force of nature. He died in Australia in 1983.

The irrefutable conclusion is that Andy and Geoffrey faced death with the monotonous regularity of a beating heart. They faced death more often and routinely than any generation since. Death accompanied them, whether in a two-man cockpit or in the decimation of a company in a trench or in the futility of charging at barbed wire and machine guns. Without such outrageous good fortune, the consequences would have been catastrophic for the continuation of their lineage. In Andy's case, his death would have prevented the birth of one hundred and thirty-one offspring. That breaks down as six children, twenty-six grandchildren, sixty-two great grandchildren and thirty-seven great great grandchildren, at the last census. I would guess the numbers on Geoffrey's account would be similar if not greater, given he had more wives than Henry the Eighth!

They say the finger of Fate is fickle and sadly this is evidenced on the other side of my family tree. One month before the end of the war, Edward Ferguson, my grandfather Jimmy Ferguson's younger brother, was killed on October 14th, 1918 aged twenty-one. He served in the 9th battalion of the Royal Irish Fusiliers, having enlisted at Greenock in Scotland where he had been working in the shipyards. He was killed during an attack on Terhan-Kezelberg in Belgium. Born in Moneyhaw near Moneymore but resident in Cookstown, he is commemorated on the Cookstown memorial. So close to the end of the war, he did not share Andy and Geoffrey's good fortune and died, like so many of these young men, without leaving a family footprint. He did leave a will dated two months before his death in what I find is a very simple but moving document.

"In the event of my death, I leave all that belongs to me to my mother. Mrs L Ferguson, Church St, Cookstown, Co. Tyrone"

All life is a miracle. As age impedes us, so understanding deepens. Findlay is the one hundred and thirty second descendant of Andy Symington. He is the first in creation to have depended on the survival of both Andrew and Geoffrey. Two young men who flaunted death, who survived, sometimes by the narrowest of margins. Findlay is the first-born son of a first-born son, of a first-born son, of a first-born son. At least! Ronnie, Anthony and Ronan welcome him to the club. Geoffrey and Andy, their glasses charged, will feel gratitude and pride that their sacrifice is still bearing fruit, over one hundred years later.

So welcome to the world, Mr Findlay Rafferty Caiger- Watson Ferguson! With the genes of Andy and Geoffrey in your bedrock, I already know you will be one amazing human being.

8. MACROECONOMIC LEGACY

In December, 1916 the War Diary of the Royal Irish Fusiliers included an intriguing note. "Germany put out peace feelers which met with no response from the Allies."

Such contemptuous rejection of the German overtures was perhaps the gravest mistake in an extensive catalogue of incompetent leadership. This one could not be pinned on the generals as it must have involved the "frocks" (a derogatory term for the politicians of the day.) The German offer of peace negotiations, to be fair, had been made quite publicly and though it contained no preconditions, it is likely they wanted to keep the land they had gained. That is probably how our political leadership read it. Ironically, their refusal to enter talks would cost far more than the comparatively small German gains- it actually cost Britain the Empire.

The decline and fall of the British Empire can be measured from December 1916. Every empire in history lost its economic power first, then followed by its military power. Thus, in late 1916, the War was costing Britain an estimated £5.5 million per day. Extending the conflict by two years led to a series of catastrophic economic consequences.

National Debt became a crippling burden. In 1913/14, the figure for National Debt was £706 million, which worked out at a manageable 26% of Gross Domestic Product (GDP). By 1918, it had risen to £7,418 million and represented 128% of GDP. Britain had transformed from a world superpower into an indebted nation. USA held much of our debt and repayment obligations helped New York replace London as the financial capital of the postwar world. The burden of repayment was magnified when Russia refused to repay loans made by Britain, arguing they were loans to the Tsar, not the people of Russia.

Waning economic power was evidenced and amplified by British adherence to the Gold Standard. Britain suspended its participation in the Gold Standard on the outbreak of the war, worried that its gold reserves would disappear (across the Atlantic). In 1914, an ounce of gold cost £3.83 in UK and $18.60 in US. This fixed an exchange rate at 4.86 between sterling and the dollar. Churchill became Chancellor of the Exchequer in 1924 and rejoined the Gold Standard at the pre-war rate of 4.86. John Maynard Keynes, the leading economist of the twentieth century, advised him the rate was too high and advised a rate of 4.4 which was ignored. The immediate impact was that British goods were overpriced by about 10%. Keynes was proved right again and exports declined rapidly.

Heavy industries like coal, steel, iron, mining and shipbuilding never recovered their pre-war positions and fell into decline. Factories were turned over to the production of munitions, so breaking their supply chain to their customers and creating a vacuum which countries like Japan quickly filled.

The biggest loss, however, was human. Around 400,000 lives were lost in the ensuing two years. Many more were invalided and some eighty thousand were declared insane, playing no further part in society. Deaths were compounded by the outbreak of Spanish Flu from 1918. In total, it was estimated that Britain and Ireland lost 1,350,000 people between 1914-18. The 1921 Census starkly captured the devastation. It recorded 109 females for every 100 males, the widest discrepancy since the first comprehensive census was taken in 1831.

Political intransigence wasted the cream of British manhood.

END OF SOMME STORY

Dramatis Personnae

The following characters have featured in Somme story:
Barbour Mary
Braden Tommy
Burns Michael ("Mickey")
Burrows A R, Brigadier General
Caiger-Watson Geoffrey, Lieut, MC OBE
Campbell Frankie
Collins Michael
Corey Barney
Corr Peter ("Petesy")
Crilly Jimmy (Publican)
Crozier Frank Percy, Brigadier General
De Ceuninck Jacques
Dexter Frank
Donaghy Joe
Doyle Willie, Father.
Ferguson Edward
Ferguson Elma
Ferguson Findlay
Ferguson Pamela
Forsyth Isabella Kennedy
Galbraith Noble
Gervin Jim Joe
Gurney Ivor
Herbert A. P. Sir, MP

Herron Mickey ("Salt")
Hughes Jim Joe ("Pan Ass")
Hunter-Weston Sir Aylmer
Kettle Thomas MP, Captain
Leckenby John George, Lieutenant
Loveband Arthur, Lieutenant Colonel
McCaughey Elma
McIlvenna Tommy
McLoughlin John
McLoughlin Thomas, Sergeant
McNally Hugh Pat
McNally John ("Montana")
Maguire Jonathan
Morgan Dessie ("Dixie")
Morgan Horsey ("the Horse")
Morgan Ned ("Cowboy")
O'Donnell Adrian ("Lugsy")
Redmond John
Robins Willie
Sassoon Siegfried
Shute Cameron Sir, Major General KCMG
Skelton Jimmy
Studdert-Kennedy Geoffrey ("Woodbine Willie")
Symington Aloysius ("Wishy")
Symington Andy
Symington Ellen (McLoughlin)
Symington Emma Teresa
Symington George ("The Barber")
Symington George Joe

Symington James
Symington Jim Charlie
Symington Lizzie (nee Forker)
Symington Madeleine
Symington Matthew ("Old Matt")
Symington Matt
Symington Matt ("Young Matt")
Symington Mary (McLoughlin)
Symington Patsy
Symington Thomas
Toner Tom

Acknowledgements

1. We are indebted to all at sirwilliamorpen.com for providing the copy of the sketch - the Exhausted Irish Fusilier at Roeux, which Sir William Orpen created on May 21st, 1917.
2. Pictures of Geoffrey Caiger- Watson are reproduced with the kind permission of his family. Thanks are owed to his granddaughter, Stephanie Caiger- Watson.
3. Pictures of the McLoughlin family are included with the kind permission of Vincent McLoughlin.
4. Thanks are owed to Jonathan Maguire, Regimental Historian at the Royal Irish Fusiliers Museum in Armagh.
5. The staff at the National Archives (TNA) at Kew for their consistent patience and support.
6. David Tattersfield of the Western Front Association for allowing the reproduction of some of his work on Pensions.
7. Monsieur Jacques de Ceuninck for his assistance and providing material on the 1918 air crash involving Geoffrey Caiger- Watson.
8. The Great War Forum whose members have provided answers, assistance and patience.
9. Taylor & Francis Group for use of Siegfried Sassoon's poem "Attack."

Epilogue (Neighbours)

As I have toiled to recollect memories of my grandfather, I have grown to appreciate what a tightly woven, communal and in the main, caring society I was fortunate to spend my childhood in. It was more a community than a society. The lack of wealth and amenities was handsomely compensated by people spending time together. The absence of telephone and television created space for storytellers and ceilidhs. People made their own entertainment and around Brackaville, they made a good job of it! Wealth and possessions have made us more insular and reserved; there were no barriers when we all had nothing. The biggest social change driver of the twenty-first century, the internet, has served to accelerate isolation and heighten barriers. Loneliness was a rare condition in the 1960s Coalisland because it simply was not allowed to exist. People were too nosey for a start!

Symingtons at 32, Derryvale Road was a ceilidh house. As was Cowboy Morgan's further up the road. The door was always open in a ceilidh house and people wanted to visit. Neighbours were drawn to them. There was no invitation, no need to knock, and no rejected entry. I can occasionally remember a stifled "Aw Jesus not him!" as some boring bastard came down the path, but even before the door closed behind him, it would be replaced by a cheery smile. "Will ye have a cup of tae?" One such miscreant was a man my father codenamed Arthur Eyetis, because of his "wailments" which included arthritis.

Nicknames were a necessity in a society where certain surnames predominate (e.g. O'Neill, Hughes, Morgan, McNally etc). Coined to aid identification, they could occasionally be cruel but also revealed the most fertile imagination. Where else could you find Pan Ass Hughes, Mary Forty Bags, Culchy Muck Carolan, Lugsy O'Donnell, Paddy Bubbly, Cowboy Morgan, Dummy Donnelly? O'Neill is the surname of Tyrone (hence the handle "the O'Neill County") and preceding nicknames abounded to differentiate one family from another. Within two square miles of the Stinkpole in Brackaville, we had the Wellpad O'Neills; Forgy, Toal; Farson, the Rebel, Rook, More, Swimmer, Yankees, Newcome, Tressies and Buffer. Apologies for those I will have missed.

The Ceilidh house would typically fill up after 9pm. Occasionally there would be music (a mouth organ or a fiddle the most popular) but mostly it would be storytelling, banter, practical jokes and always "tae"! Tea served with delicacies like soda bread, potato bread, potato apple bread, toasted pan loaf, fried tomato bread, tomato sandwiches, homemade "wee buns" and apple tarts. If there had been a win on the horses, the menu was enhanced with fare from the bread man, including snowballs and currant squares, a particular favourite of mine from the Kennedy bread van. At 10pm exactly, the hubbub would be guillotined by a silence rivalled only by the "Eyes down, first number" call in a bingo hall. The radio was switched on, the news headlines endured impatiently until we got to the meat of the matter…the Racing Roundup! With the racing pages of the Irish News and pen in hand, my grandfather would systematically mark the winners, second and third, with starting prices, as dockets from Gerry Herron's "bookey shop" were meticulously examined by the gathered throng. Andy's wife, Lizzie, would often provide commentary: "that hoor Piggot", "Joe Mercer is a crook" and "God bless Scobie Breasley". "Shut your mouth, I can't hear!" would generate a collective, rasping shush as silence was instantly restored. Sometimes it was the last remark preceding pandemonium. The Shipping Forecast would sound in the background as the racing results were digested.

"Forties, Cromarty, Forth…"

"Did anybody hear how Brigadier Gerard did in the 3.30 at Ascot?"

"Dogger, Fisher, German Bight…"

"It didn't win."

"Thames, Dover…"

"I know it didn't fucking win, did it run?"

This question was as serious as anything asked in Parliament that day. It could be the difference between two winners on a losing treble (bad luck, no return) or a winning double (can you lend me five bob)? As the Shipping forecast headed off to Southeast Iceland via Faeroes, I would be despatched to Jim Skelton's to establish the fate of Brigadier Gerard. Jim Skelton was an authority on Racing SPs (Starting Prices). A retired, former miner, every day at around 5pm he would don his bicycle clips and cycle down to Gerry Herron's in the 'Island. I did not know what a photographic memory was, but everybody knew Jim had one, tucked under his cloth cap. Especially when it came to "the results." Jim would pronounce judgement on the Brigadier, then go through the quite unnecessary task of checking it in his assiduously marked up newspaper. He lived next door to Paddy McArdle, a spit from Crilly's, so my errand often extended to buying a packet (ten) of Woodbine, Park Drive, Players, Embassy or Kensitas, depending on who was visiting that night.

An evening in the ceilidh house typically featured an excess of people in a small living room, conducting an array of sometimes conflicting activities. Guests sat on the settee, trying to drink tea while Wishy ferreted around under their feet, looking for his football boots and in the middle of it all, my mother doing the ironing. In the six weeks preceding Easter, there would invariably be a collective Lenten call to the Rosary. This would cause the assembled throng to fall to their knees and face the wall where they could admire framed colour pictures of John F Kennedy and Pope John XXIII. Back-turned and hunched over a chair left the prayer in a vulnerable position. And increased the capacity for mischief to irresistible levels. Paddy Bubbly's Holy Mary response won him immortality in our family folklore: "Holy Mary Mother of God agghhh Fuck!" as an impish Emma Teresa pressed her hot iron against his ass. My grandmother Lizzie was more devout than Andy, but he maintained a dignified reverence, nonetheless. Unfortunately, their backs being turned made supervision impossible. Improvised missiles proliferated, a well-aimed wet, tea towel often inducing a communal burst of coughing in a tonsil-swallowing attempt to strangle laughter at source. Responsibility for leading the Rosary would transfer with each Joyful Mystery. Uncle Patsy held the lap record for a decade of the Rosary, employing the device of starting the next Hail Mary while the respondents were half-way through their response to the former, then running the words together like an auctioneer on speed. "Pray for us sinners" always triggered a real-time response from Patsy's accelerating Hail Mary, like a racing car exiting the chicane.

Another lasting memory of this bygone era was the storytelling. I remember the aforementioned Montana as a man who could hold an audience and weave a story, in the noble tradition of the seanchaí who preceded him. The seanchaí were travelling storytellers who travelled from village to village and house to house. In return for a meal or a night's shelter, they would tell their stories. For many centuries, they were not just storytellers but custodians of tradition, history, mythology and heritage- they played a vital role in an Ireland dependent on an oral culture. Montana let none of them down. This diminutive man, sat on the edge of a chair with his cap on one knee since it was disrespectful to wear a cap indoors, he would hold the room in thrall. Delivering his tale, the only competition for his voice was the pendulum clock on the far wall. His words seemed to hang in the air. The impact was almost hypnotic. When he finished, it was like being woken from a trance. The recall to mindfulness rippled across the audience like a wave. It was a unique experience and although television replaced it, the paradox is that television will never replace it.

One behavioural oddity has resurfaced in my memory. When we wanted a friend to come out to play, the protocol was to gather at his front gate and from there, shout his name. "Dessie!!" It was like there had been mines laid along his garden path. No-one would venture beyond the gate. The shout would be repeated every fifteen seconds or so until a curtain twitched, and the required face would signal availability. If a game of football was being set up, my house was nearest the football stadium and an assembled posse would call my name in unison "Ant-knee!" An array of varying talents stood in wait, including McGlone, Morgan, McNally, Burns, Gates, Day(s) et al.

The football "stadium" was called "The Hollow," a field backing the council houses opposite. Unfortunately, it was also a farmer's field which could cause problems on match day. One Lugsy O'Donnell kept his cows in the Hollow, but these could be easily shewed into a corner as the pitch was prepared for action- four piles of coats laid down, each signifying a goalpost. One touchline was the barbed wire that ran along the back gardens, the opposite touchline was open to negotiation, though it was generally considered to be about halfway up the hill towards a "hollowed" out former sandpit- hence "the Hollow". Two captains would be appointed, and the teams picked alternately from the assembled talent, in descending order of ability. Game on!

Lugsy O'Donnell lived a couple of miles away and was usually unavailable for interference. I don't think he liked football. He probably was not very sporting, and he definitely did not like vandals trampling the grass that was the preserve of his precious cows! Warnings had gone unheeded. Lugsy decided to take the law into his own hands...the game was finely poised at 9-8 and with time running out, I trotted over to take a corner at the Mill Row end as every attacker, defender and passing card cheat formed an expectant crowd around a nervous goalkeeper. As I picked up the ball, I didn't know that corner would never be taken...

The explosion shocked me. I looked back in stupefaction as the goalmouth melee evaporated at high speed in all directions. Sanctuary urgently required! As Lugsy discharged the second barrel of his shotgun, Dessie Morgan and I simultaneously vaulted Ernie Fulton's fence. To this day, I regret that my run from the corner had gone untimed. Was it really inside the Olympic qualifying time- we will never know? Enjoying diplomatic immunity behind the cover of Fulton's hedge, Dessie and I surveyed the scene over the Hollow. Only three actors remained on stage. Lugsy, gun in hand, striding purposefully to claim his prisoners.

Awaiting him, Mickey Burns and Frankie Campbell, arms raised in surrender! As Leonard Cohen sang: "they were reaching for the sky just to surrender." Cowardice, capitulation and capture- they were guilty on all counts. Over 50 years later, we still rib them about it.

Looking back from our enriched perch in the twenty-first century, the lack of amenities at our disposal was remarkable. Apart from a public call box on Main Street in Coalisland, the only telephone in Brackaville was in Maggie Corey's house. The nearest swimming pool was Roughan Lough. We played football on the Hollow, not to annoy Lugsy, but because it was the only vaguely level patch of ground within two square miles! Even Brackaville Owen Roes GFC played at Mullaghmoyle on what was really another farmer's field. Tom Toner was unique in owning a leather case football. I can still smell the leather now and remember the tube inside it, which had more patches than our Nial's arms when he stopped smoking. Whether through frugality or impecuniosity, Tom's penchant for patching things up extended to his football boots, which were a collection of holes and rips held together by bits of string, gut, and stitching. At fifteen, I made my (goal scoring) debut for Brackaville Seniors away at Moortown. On the bus down, Petesie Corr's eyes fell upon Tom's boots, cueing the immortal proclamation:

"Tom, if you were hanged for wearing football boots, you would die innocent!"

With thirty per cent unemployment, there was an active black economy which provided labour on a cash only basis. Those "drawing the brew" (vernacular for people on benefits from the Employment Bureau), could supplement their income by casual labour which in itself stimulated employment: "the Brew men" were a team of fraud investigators who could set pulses (and legs) racing with an unexpected visit to a remote workplace. One man who could put the casual into labour was Parley Jackson. My uncle Wishy worked for Dan Carolan, a tarmac contractor from Galway originally, who was known as "Culchy Muck." I have no idea why. My grandfather had commissioned Culchy Muck to lay some tarmac on the drive. The day dawned and the team duly arrived. Wishy, a sedulous, prodigious worker, was spreading and rolling while Dan shovelled the tarmac from the lorry into the wheelbarrow. In this endeavour, he was assisted by Parley, who fancied a day's wages. There the duo toiled, one each side of the barrow. Concerned about Parley's productivity (in the Tyrone colloquialism-"the dead lice were dropping off him"), Dan exhorted Parley to greater efforts.

"Dan, I am shovelling against my hand," Parley explained.

"Parley, you are shovelling against your will!"

One of the social highlights of the year was the Annual Guest Tea held at the Parochial Centre. In return for purchasing a ticket, diners would squeeze into long, unbroken rows of tables to enjoy the fare. Sandwiches, buns, cakes, and biscuits washed down with multiple cups of tae. It was a bit like an early smorgasbord- you could eat all you wanted, but you couldn't even have carried home all you were offered. Strictly no alcohol, though. The hubbub of excited chatter and the clinking of china cups on saucers kept the decibel level high. In a town that had only two "restaurants" (Landi's and McGlinchey's chip shops), the Guest Tea was La Dolce Vita. No matter that the tea could vary on a Richter scale from hot water to tannin stew, depending on the gap between brewing and serving.

This was an innocent time: spaghetti came in hoops from a tin, and no-one had heard of pizza. An Indian was Lal Singh. Curry was a boy from Edendork. When the feeding frenzy abated, the crowning moment...you get your picture taken! Rows of smiling faces, name tagged and faithfully reproduced the following Thursday in the Democrat. Photographs needed developing, so people had to be patient. No previews and no

"Delete" key. The first time you knew your eyes were closed in the picture was on Thursday, simultaneously when the world saw it in that coveted edition. And that was it- none of us would drink from china for another year.

No money, no infrastructure, no facilities, no investment- yet mainly happy people, a caring community and some terrific characters! There was one sport where the town was well provided for: snooker. St Patrick's Hall had a table upstairs, and Gervin's had eight tables. Apart from Gaelic football, snooker was the most popular sport in the town. A young Dennis Taylor honed his skills at Gervin's under the watchful mentoring of Jim Joe, and a decade or so later, Taylor reached the apotheosis of his career, when he became Coalisland's one and only world champion, after a titanic struggle with Steve Davis.

Jim Joe Gervin merits a pause in our story. He holds a deserved place in Coalisland's pantheon of characters. Patrolling the snooker hall in a brown shopkeeper's coat, this old man maintained order on his ship in a rebellious ocean of chaos. Squat, swarthy, bulbous lipped and sporting the unruly remnants of a former head of curls, Jim Joe's deep voice would boom out, pinpointing a misdemeanour at the opposite end of the hall, freezing the culprit in mid-perpetration. Everyone knew he had eyes in the back of his head. He was so sharp that some thought him stupid, in the same way the tabloids maligned Prince Philip in later years. I thumbed a book once many years ago: "the Witticisms of Prince Philip". Believe me it had nothing on the "sayings of Jim Joe Gervin". As an example, we had a colloquialism, "to be black with" which expressed abundance. The field was black with rabbits; the river was black with trout. Following a Humphrey Bogart film in the Fifties, every sharp dude in Coalisland sported a white raincoat. Rain or shine, you had to be seen in one to "look the part". The fashion was not lost on Jim Joe, who pronounced that the town was "black with white raincoats". Deadpan delivery caused some to laugh at an old fool. The joke was on them…

From the pantheon of characters, the Horse Morgan comes into my head. I doubt if the word "doppelganger" had ever been used in Coalisland of the 1960s. If it had, it could only have been in the context of Alfred Hitchcock and Horsey Morgan. They were doppelgangers! Bald, corpulent beyond rotund and housed in an old dark suit, they were a pair of rare birds indeed. Horsey had been the town's tailor for many years and lived in a house at the bottom of Barrack Row opposite Saint Patrick's Hall. The house afforded commanding views: up Barrack Street beyond McCaffreys shop and Father Walls torture chamber, down Main Street past Mamies' Corner to Kelly's Yard and diagonally across the Square. It was a strategic perch, ideal for an arch predator. Like Hitchcock, the Horse had a sense of drama and the opportunities it could bring. One day, he burst into Seamie Dorman's bar in the Square, looking pale, upset and flustered. "Quick! Quick! Brandy! A woman has fainted outside". Keen to discharge his social responsibilities, the young barman passed over a generous shot of Martell which Horsey immediately took from him and necked in one, unbroken movement. As the colour returned to his cheeks, he explained: "I hate to see a woman faint!" A free drink and a place in legend.

I struggle to think of Coalisland and its characters without reference to my father, Ronnie. Generous, quick-witted and fun loving, he was a popular figure around the town. A man who could hold a tune, he was always in demand as a compere and often "strutted the boards" at the Parochial Centre. His humour was sharp and occasionally, could be brutal. Decrying the efforts of a less than handy handyman, he created the ultimate put-down:

"that man couldn't bless himself without scratching his face!"

His quick wit also manifest itself at home, where my younger siblings had to remain alert to avoid becoming the unwanted butt of humour. I remember a ten-year-old Judy, always eager to please, setting a plate of freshly buttered toast on the kitchen table.

"Who buttered this toast?" inquired my father.

"I did!" volunteered Judy, keen to harvest any gratitude on offer.

"Who scraped it off again?"

Cue convulsions of laughter in the Ferguson family, including Judy herself.

Happy days. Despite almost fifty years in exile, I still call Coalisland "home." And proud to do so.

Jim "the Horse" Morgan

Montana (c1975)

Parley Jackson & Ronnie Ferguson

Patsy Symington (c1954)

Somme Story Reviews

Andy Symington: Tyrone's Most Wanted Man is a series containing three books. The first book in the series is Somme Story, originally published in 2022. This edition of the Somme Story has been extended and updated in 2025. Below is a selection of reviews left by readers on Amazon, where the book has over 30 reviews and enjoys a star rating of 4.6 out of 5.

"Brilliant story telling based on facts. An easy-to-read book which brings history to life." M.A. Quinn

"Excellent read which tells the human story of the impact of WW1 on the lives of those who fought and subsequent impact on their families. Amid the harrowing futility of army strategy, the book is interspersed with humour and is a light and fast-paced read. Lucidly covers the complex issues of war, poverty and social unrest." Fergy

"Fine characterisation. Offers a good insight into early 20th century culture. Humour is deftly contrasted with the profound misery of war" Gert Cavaradossi

"I read this absorbing book with great interest because it revealed the reality of combat as

witnessed by ordinary soldiers. What they had to face, how they endured appalling conditions and were led by incompetent generals, and how futile war was and still is. A great contribution with insightful opinions which pull no punches."
Steve C.

"Tony Ferguson set out to write about his grandfather Andy Symington and his life growing up and surviving WW1 and the Somme in this first of 3 books. Very readable and excellent descriptions that make you feel the horrors Andy and all servicemen must have felt. It covers the ineptitude of those in charge and the long term effects of "shell shock." Would definitely read the next instalment of Andy's incredible life and if you are interested in WW1 would certainly recommend."
Sheila

"This book is enlightening and entertaining. The author remains objective despite his affection for the protagonists. The social and economic conditions that led to rural Irishmen enlisting in the British Army during World War I are well described; just enough information on world events helps the reader follow the action."
James O'Mahoney

"It is a rewarding read and highly recommended."
Bob Goodwin

"Masterfully written and thoroughly researched. A story that leaves you wanting more. I thoroughly enjoyed this book."
Libby Campbell

"A read to put you through all the emotions- sadness, anger and great humour. Extremely well written with a final chapter worth waiting for"
RF Watson

"A wonderful read- appealing to those that like first world war stories but also a heartwarming look back at life in Ireland in the last century."
Karen

"Well written, eloquent and erudite."
Judy Wilson

"The First World War prose is as good as any I've read on the subject and deeply affecting. The surprising twist of fate as the story unfolds is a joy to discover." Debbie

"Great read. Would highly recommend this book."
Elma McCaughey

All the above reviews have been taken from Amazon.co.uk

Reviews by other Authors

A thoroughly researched, well written and unique account of the life of the author's grandfather, a resolute Ulsterman who met the intense demands and challenges of his times with determination and fortitude. This moving story, told with obvious admiration, is remarkable for an amazing twist of fate which links events of World War One with the family's newest generation.
Denise Beddows, award-winning author of True Crime Award nominated 'The Forgotten Forty-Four' and 'The Wronged Man'.

"What makes this book both compelling and unique is the way that the author skilfully and beautifully blends the harsh facts of the times and places with the extremely personal perspective of his grandfather. For me it was an emotional rollercoaster that allowed me to gain a real insight into the realities of World War One, the Battle of the Somme in particular, and the very personal insights of a young Irish soldier. The research behind the book is impressive and graphically sets the scene for the consequent horror, pathos and dark trench humour that unfurls as the pages turn. The obvious deep bond between author and his grandfather shines through. It is an apt reminder of the horrors of war but also of the triumph of the human spirit. A truly wonderful book. I'm really looking forward to the next two books about Andy Symington."

Allan MacGregor Author, Absence of Certainty

Ferguson takes what some will assume to be a dry subject and infuses it with emotion, detail and a fresh, heartfelt perspective on the challenges faced by a proud Tyrone man plunged into the chaos of Europe at war. Meticulous research brings the history, and the ancestor involved vividly to life. A powerhouse of historical writing to be relished at each turn of the page.

J.A.Marley, Author, The Danny Felix Thrillers and The Planted Trilogy.

A combination of personal investment (Tony Ferguson is writing about his grandfather); a penchant for stubborn (and rewarding) genealogical research; and a deep interest in military history give this story about a remarkable Irishman its passion and its realism.

Ed Peile, Author, Emeritus Professor of Medical Education in the University of Warwick Medical School

Photographs

A young Andy Symington

Andy c.1926

Thomas McLoughlin (seated)

Andy & Madeleine 1962

Mary McLoughlin (nee Symington). Dolly bottom left

Medal Card. SWB is the Silver War Badge

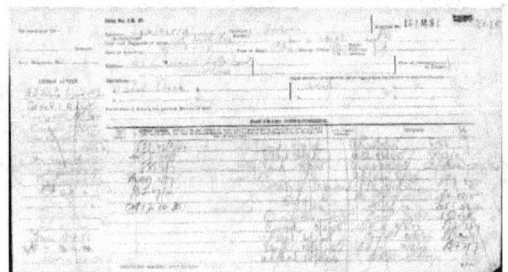

Pension Card(s)

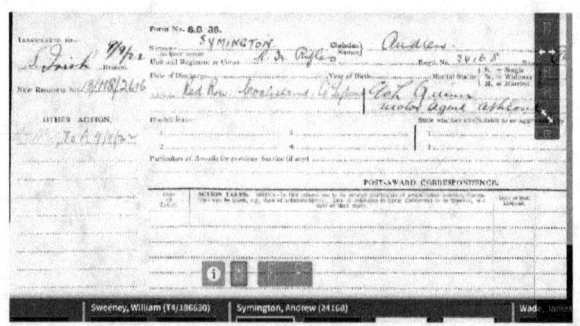

Last Will and Testament of Private Edward Ferguson

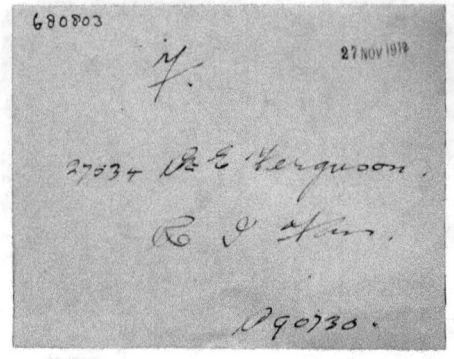
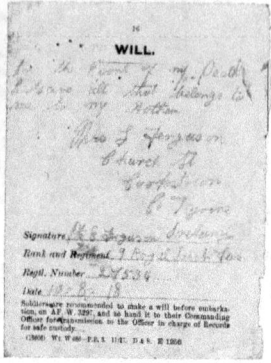

Edward Ferguson's grave at Dadizeele British Cemetry, Belgium

Lieutenant Geoffrey Caiger-Watson

Geoffrey Caiger-Watson in RFC 1918

French newspaper report

Author

Andrew James Anthony (a.k.a "Tony") Ferguson left his native Tyrone in September 1973, bound for the East Riding of Yorkshire. He earned a B.Sc in Economics at the University of Hull, sparking a lifelong love affair with "the Tigers" of Hull City AFC.

He worked for over forty years in technology, holding several international management positions with global corporations- Burroughs, Unisys and Accenture. He has been published many times in his specialist fields: the application of technology in banking and insurance.

An accomplished and charismatic speaker, he regularly gives talks on a range of historical subjects, including the Somme and the Irish War of Independence.

"Somme Story" is the first book in the trilogy of "Andy Symington: Tyrone's Most Wanted Man" series.

E-Mail the author
If you would like to be informed on progress with the other two volumes in the trilogy, please leave your e-mail address with the author: tony@ibl.ie

Andy Symington: Tyrone's Most Wanted Man
Volume 2: Irish War of Independence

Andy Symington: Tyrone's Most Wanted Man
Volume 3: Irish Civil War

www.ingramcontent.com/pod-product-compliance
Lightning Source LLC
Chambersburg PA
CBHW052030070526
44584CB00016B/1983